Children with Reading Problems: A Guidebook for Parents

2nd Edition

Ruth Rogers Erickson
Edsel L. Erickson

LEARNING PUBLICATIONS, INC.
Box 1326
Holmes Beach, Florida 33509

Learning Publications, Inc.
P.O. Box 1326
Holmes Beach, Florida 33509

Designed by Darryl Pfau

Library of Congress Catalog Card Number 76-58796

Hardback: 0-918452-11-2
Paperback: 0-918452-12-0

Printing: 1 2 3 4 5 6 7 8   Year: 9 0 1 2 3 4

Printed in the United States of America

ACKNOWLEDGEMENTS

Our appreciation must go to many persons for making this book possible. We owe Ruth Park and Joseph Chapel a special thanks for their many editorial and substantive contributions. We also wish to thank Jean Bournazos, Barbara McFadden and Judith Brawer for their assistance in preparing the manuscript and Annlee Decent, Charles Burket, Kimon Bournazos and Lee Joiner for their professional support and criticism.

We are perhaps most indebted to the many parents and teachers with whom we have worked in their homes and schools over the past 20 years who must go unnamed but who provided the testing ground and motivation for this book.

CONTENTS

PART A

INTRODUCTION

Helping Your Child to Read:
You Can and You Should

If you are the parent of a school age child with a reading problem, the most important thing for you to realize is that *you can be of help, or you can make matters worse.* While no normal parent wants to increase a child's difficulties, sometimes eagerness to help (without proper preparation, skills and attitudes) can result in just that.

In this chapter you will review six areas that we have found important in creating a successful home atmosphere for helping children to be better readers. These areas concern:

- Becoming Properly Prepared
- Your Responsibilities as a Tutor
- Your Attitudes Toward Teachers
- How to Work with Teachers
- Avoiding Embarrassment
- Controlling Anxiety and Being Confident

BE PREPARED

When you are organized and prepared in your approach to helping your child and have your day-to-day activities scheduled, you will find your frustrations and anxieties disappearing. Without careful planning, your help may be "hit or miss," and thus ineffective. There is little wonder that parent help-sessions often end in shouting matches or in pent-up resentments, with the child even more frustrated than the parent.

In this book we will try to help you understand the nature of the reading process; the work of teachers and parents; reasons for reading failures; and how you can help your son or daughter to become a better reader. We believe that most parents who follow our suggestions will discover they can bring about higher levels of school achievement without creating undue anxieties in either their children or themselves.

ASSUME THE RESPONSIBILITY

Many parents mistakenly believe that teaching their child to read better is not their responsibility; they assume that only teachers should teach reading, or that there is nothing they can do that will get results. Unfortunately, some educators have contributed to this attitude by suggesting a hands-off approach as far as school work is concerned. As a result, many parents have been discouraged from participating in the schooling of their children. "Just send us a happy and perhaps a gifted child and we will do the rest," seems to express the attitude of some educators.

Nevertheless, many parents have not been turned away from their responsibility to assist in the educational growth of their offspring. Every day, parents are successfully listening to their youngsters read; they are successfully encouraging reading; and they are helping their children to develop improved reading skills and interests.

There is no doubt that teachers have taught millions of students to read with little or no assistance from parents. Clearly, our schools have served millions of children very well. Indeed, scores of thousands of children—poor and rich alike—have learned to read in school with little teaching assistance from parents.

However, not all children have been so lucky. In many students' cases, teachers could use and would welcome the help of parents and others. If your youngster is having trouble with reading, it is your responsibility to inform yourself so that you will be effective in providing needed assistance.

AVOID BLAMING TEACHERS

Even when you believe teachers have not been as successful as they ought to have been, avoid blaming the school for failing to teach your child to be a good reader. No child will become a successful reader simply because the family lives in a "good" neighborhood, sends their child to a supposedly "superior" school, and provides a loving and supportive home background. We have heard parents lament, "We bought a house in this neighborhood so our child could go to a good school. Why didn't he learn to read as we were sure he would?" We have also heard parents express the regret that their children were attending a supposedly "inferior" school.

We know that teachers make a big difference in the development of children, and that teachers vary considerably in their skill to teach reading. We also know that the majority of teachers get excellent results with most students—and that there are numerous causes of reading disability in children. Nevertheless, there are many ways of helping nearly all children to read better, regardless of circumstances. The foremost point to keep in mind is that once you have an accurate idea of the nature of your child's difficulties, there usually are concrete steps you can take to help.

Over the years we have worked with hundreds of parents who have learned to help their children become better readers. We have worked in the public schools as teachers; as specialists in university remedial reading and learning research centers; as school psychologists; and as evaluators of reading programs in many parts of the country.

LEARN HOW TO WORK WITH TEACHERS

Classroom teachers and parents frequently ask us to evaluate a particular student who is having reading problems. After we complete an evaluation and have come to some conclusions about the nature of the student's difficulties, we discuss our findings with the child's teacher and parents. From our experience, we have learned how little time the typical classroom teacher has to deal with an individual child's reading problems. In addition, we have discovered that often there are few specialized reading resources available to teachers—even within many so-called upper or middle-class schools. Recognizing these problems, we have often found it necessary to turn to the child's parents for providing the time and attention the child's problems demand. And who has a greater vested interest in a child's achievement than that child's parents?

We generally find that parents are sympathetic to their children's problems, but that often they become frustrated when attempting to be of help. Some parents come to dread parent conferences with each new teacher, since they believe they can predict before they get to school the negative comments the teacher is going to make. Frequently, parents ignore requests for conferences, feeling that nothing they can do will resolve their child's problem.

Also, while many parents are told a child needs parental help with reading, they are not told exactly how to go about helping. As a result, parents often needlessly pay hundreds of dollars to unprofessional tutors, or anyone else they think might be able to help their child. After such parents are shown how to approach remedial reading and are encouraged to try it, they are able to work with their children successfully.

Naturally, some reluctance on the part of parents results from genuine concern that their efforts to help may only cause confusion or interfere with their youngster's progress in school. However, children benefit markedly when their parents and teachers are working together.

DO NOT COMMUNICATE EMBARRASSMENT

Do not feel embarrassed or guilty if your son or daughter has a reading problem. At the very least, you should make a strong attempt to resist communicating such feelings—either to your child or to other members of the family.

You should remember that reading failure occurs among children from widely different backgrounds. It occurs among those from warm, loving and supportive families as well as among those who have been neglected. Reading failures occur among children from both intact and broken homes; from upper, middle, and lower class families; and among children from homes in which the mother works and homes in which the mother does not work.

Also, children with reading problems vary widely in personality—the shy or the aggressive, the withdrawn or the outgoing, the carefree or the anxious—all can have difficulties with reading.

AVOID ANXIETY AND SHOW CONFIDENCE

Our recommendation is that you do not become overly anxious about your child's reading problems. Any fears and anxieties you may have must be controlled—even though this may be extremely difficult for you to do at times.

If you tend to be overly anxious, this book should be of help. Fears and anxieties are usually the consequence of not understanding a situation, or of not knowing what to do in specific situations.

Remember—You Are Important. Reading is a skill nearly all youngsters must learn, one way or another. It is taught by many different methods, and we have yet to see any one method that works for everyone. Reading is a skill taught directly and indirectly, knowingly and unknowingly, by many different people. There is no reason why you as a parent should not be one of those people. You can and you should be a positive force in the life of your child.

SUMMARY

In this chapter we discussed the six most common pitfalls to helping your child. Be certain that you have studied them carefully. It will help if you review this chapter from time to time. Ask yourself the following questions when dealing with your child:

1. Am I *always prepared* when helping my child?

2. Do I assume *responsibility* with the school for my child's reading problems?

3. Do I *blame* the teacher or do I pitch in and help?

4. Am I taking an active and positive approach in learning how to *work with teachers*?

5.   Do I show *embarrassment* or guilt feelings when helping my child? Do I take a positive approach?

6.   Do I *control* my fears and anxieties? Do I show *confidence*?

It takes hard work to create a working environment in which your child will improve. It can be done if you periodically review these pitfalls.

2

Seeking Help

A child with reading problems should be examined by specialists or experts whose training has enabled them to pinpoint causes for an individual's lack of achievement. Routine physical and educational screening examinations given in school are helpful but are not always thorough enough. Some youngsters have physical, emotional, social and instructional impairments which are subtle and difficult to discern. In this chapter you will learn about the role and importance of experts in dealing with:

- Vision and Hearing Problems

- Physical Needs

- Psychological and Social Handicaps

- Special Reading and Learning Disabilities

It is important for you to determine the source of your child's difficulty if you wish to increase your chances of helping him or her to become a better reader.

YOUR CHILD'S VISION

Have your child's vision checked by an ophthalmologist or optometrist. It may be that your child is not seeing letters and words clearly. Types of visual problems which may interfere with reading are: *hyperopia* (farsightedness), *myopia* (nearsightedness), and *astigmatism* (blurring of vision due to a defect in the eye).

Hyperopia

The child with hyperopia sees better at a distance than at close range. Farsighted children typically seek to avoid close reading as well as written work at their seats. The teacher may not be aware of this visual problem (since such children can read from the chalkboard) and may suspect the pupil of avoiding assignments. To compound this situation, such pupils may, by straining their eyes, see close work reasonably well for a short time. Parents have additional difficulty noticing farsightedness because their children can sit back and watch television without any apparent difficulty. This subtle visual problem can be detected and corrected by an ophthalmologist or optometrist. The greatest problem may be to get the farsighted child to wear his or her glasses for close work.

Myopia

On the other hand, the myopic child is easily identified through the type of visual screening that is commonly done at school. This child has difficulty seeing at a distance. The nearsighted child usually squints in order to see the chalkboard and sits quite close to the television at home. Glasses certainly help a child with this type of eye difficulty, and the nearsighted child will usually wear his glasses without too much prodding.

Astigmatism

Astigmatism is not readily identified through the normal vision screening at school. If a child complains of blurred vision, an eye specialist should be consulted. This type of visual problem may result in the child being unable to distinguish between similar letters or numbers, such as *b* and *d, p* and *g, m* and *n,* or *3* and *8.* Astigmatism can also be corrected by glasses.

Other Vision Problems

There are many other types of visual problems. Muscle imbalance (crossed eyes), cateracts, and glaucoma are possible in children, but the three conditions described above are the most common visual difficulties found in the young. Any visual problem should be diagnosed and corrected as quickly as possible. To wait too long will only cause your child pain, discomfort, confusion, and a definite loss of valuable instruction time at school and at home.

YOUR CHILD'S HEARING

Have your child's hearing checked by an audiologist. In many cities there are speech and hearing clinics that provide this service at little or no cost. You may have been unable to detect a hearing problem because your child has learned to compensate for hearing loss by pretending, lipreading, or some other method. A child must be able to hear sounds as accurately as possible. Some characteristics of the child with a hearing loss are:

1. Facial contortions or blank expressions;

2. Responding inappropriately to spoken directions when unable to see the face of the speaker;

3. Complaints of inattentiveness from the child's teacher or others;

4. Excessive responses of "sir," "huh?," "what," and similar indications of not hearing requests;

5. Obvious clues such as turning an car toward the speaker, or putting a hand behind an ear in order to gain a better understanding of what is being said;

6. Generally poor school achievement because of inability to understand many of the directions; and

7. Difficulty in recognizing differences between sounds, especially such sounds as those made by the letters *b, t* and *d* or *m* and *n.*

An audiologist can almost always detect the difficulties and recommend what should be done.

Ear Infections

Should an audiologist fail to find any physical impairment, you must still be alert to possible hearing problems. Watch for ear infections and colds. Some children have trouble hearing only during an illness. There are children who have passed hearing tests, then have become ill with ear infections that cause hearing loss. During this period, the child is not able to pay proper attention to directions at school and is easily distracted.

There are many children whose ears must be drained on a regular basis. If a child's ear passages tend to become clogged frequently, watch for periods when he or she does not respond normally to sound or voices; it may be time for a trip to the doctor's office. The child's teacher should also be made aware of this condition so that intervals of inadequate responses at school can be reported to you. Teachers sometimes identify symptoms of illness not recognized by parents. This happened in the following case of Kim, a first grader:

Kim was shy and withdrawn with her teacher and the other children in the classroom. She was not learning to read even though she had high achievement scores in her kindergarten tests. In the teachers' lounge one day, the first grade teacher was puzzling about Kim, and the child's former kindergarten teacher overheard her comments. "You cannot possibly be talking about Kim B___ , the happy and outgoing child I knew last year," she said.

As a result of this conversation with the previous teacher, Kim's first grade teacher decided to ask the child's mother to come to school.

Kim's mother said she suspected a hearing problem, but had "not gotten around to" taking her to a doctor since Kim had not made any serious complaints at home. Fortunately, the next day her problem was quickly diagnosed by an ear specialist as a recurrence of a middle ear infection, and the little girl was quickly helped back to good health and good performance in school.

A teacher asked us to observe a child in her room. She stated that on some days the child literally screamed at her and the other pupils, and learned very little. On other days, when the child was quiet, she seemed to learn rapidly.

One of the things we did was to stand behind the child and talk to her in a normal tone. She made no response at all. We immediately suspected that she was not hearing correctly and called a speech and hearing center for an emergency appointment with an audiologist. The results of the examination revealed that the girl had a severe hearing loss in her right ear and that the hearing in her left ear was not completely normal.

We suspected that this child, like Kim, might have a middle ear infection which would cause her hearing to be better on some days than on others. An ear specialist was called. The doctor cleared up the infection, and later the audiologist fitted the youngster's right ear with a hearing aid. These corrective measures had dramatic results in the form of a happier and more alert child, who rapidly became capable of normal classroom performance.

Listening and Conversing

Children with hearing problems usually need special help in listening. You can teach your hard-of-hearing child, or any child, to be a good listener yourself. If your child is deaf or hard of hearing, it is especially important that you and others regularly carry on long conversations with him or her. These conversations should focus on events and people of interest to the child.

Avoid emphasizing (or perhaps even discussing) reading or hearing problems. Pay full attention to your child's interests without acting like a judge. Subtly try to get him or her to tell you what happened during the day without appearing inquisitive; discuss what he or she liked or disliked about school that day. Read stories and talk about them; ask for and openly show respect for your child's opinions—even when they differ from your own.

Remember, when you talk to the hard-of-hearing, young or old, make sure that you have the person's attention. Try to make good eye contact and talk normally. An audiologist or a speech pathologist can give excellent and specific advice for improving communication with a hard-of-hearing person.

YOUR CHILD'S PHYSICAL HEALTH

Physical Examination

Your child should also have a thorough physical examination by a physician. Some children are tired and listless most of the day in school. They do not have sufficient energy to get through a school day successfully, thus little work is accomplished. A physician may check for thyroid abnormalities. A child with hyperthyroidism will be over-active and irritable, and will tire easily; the child with hypothyroidism will be underactive and will tend to be overweight and sluggish. Other kinds of thyroid imbalance can cause learning problems.

Allergies

Allergies cause other physical conditions that can drain a person's energy but they may not be easily recognized except by an allergist. Many parents and teachers are unaware of their children's allergies, mistaking allergic reactions for colds or flu.

An example of the allergic child was furnished by Tim, a sixth grade student who had little interest in school. He did not participate in sports or other school related activities and he was quite overweight for his age. He was often absent from school because of what appeared to be a series of colds. When in school, he frequently had his head on his desk. His eyes sometimes watered and he occasionally had a rash around his mouth. The school psychologist and reading specialist found Tim to be extremely intelligent, but at a reading level approximately two years below his actual grade placement. Both experts also reported that it was difficult for Tim to complete their tests because of apparent fatigue and sluggishness.

Tim's mother expressed sincere concern, but was at a loss as to what to do. She had taken Tim to their family doctor, a general practitioner, who reported him to be in normal health. Since we had seen similar cases, one of our first questions to Tim's mother was, "Have you ever taken him to an allergist?" She replied, "I'll try anything," and immediately called her family doctor for a recommendation to a specialist in allergies.

The allergist, on examining the boy, found him to be highly allergic to milk, soda pop, flour, tomatoes, and other things he had been eating for many years. When Tim was given a diet free of these foods, his cold symptoms decreased; in addition, a remarkable improvement in learning occurred. Not only did the boy's face clear up and his sluggishness disappear, he began to take an active interest in school. His reading quickly improved as be began to read more. Consequently, his parents and teachers were more capable of giving him the added help he needed.

Rest and Nutrition

For most children, learning to read is a task demanding considerable energy; therefore, it is essential for them to be physically well, alert, and attentive. You will need to be sure that your child receives plenty of rest and a proper diet.

PSYCHOLOGICAL AND SOCIAL SERVICES

Perhaps you should have your child examined by a school psychologist or school social worker. If services of school psychologists, counselors or social workers are available in your school district, the type of services offered will depend on their training and experience. In some school districts, counselors, school psychologists and social workers have had extensive training in reading diagnosis and prescriptive instruction.

Actually, results depend on the skills available among all staff members. Some school psychologists are expected merely to administer intelligence tests; others are expected to provide only consultation services to teachers. In some localities, school systems hire psychometrists who administer psychological tests, plus school psychologists who receive these test results and interpret them to parents and teachers. There are also school psychologists who are more concerned about the emotional health of students than about their reading achievement.

Contact Your Child's School

Contact your child's teacher or principal to determine what kind of psychological and social services your child needs and can expect.

Most school psychologists are equipped to administer and interpret a variety of tests measuring intelligence, reading, spelling, and arithmetic achievement, perceptual skills, and vocational interests. In addition they are often trained to provide an assessment of the social and emotional conditions associated with learning failure.

Following is a typical example of how one school psychologist partially described a student's social and emotinal situation in school:

"Bobby's teacher decided after one month of school that she needed help with him. He came to school the first day upset and crying because of a fight on the bus. Mrs. T____ , his new second grade teacher, talked to Bobby and calmed him down for a while, but he spent an unhappy day at school. His early morning altercation continued during recess and at lunch. The second day of school was better, but he was easily upset when the boy next to him accidentally bumped him. When assignments were given to the class and the teacher was ready for her reading group, Bobby shouted that he didn't know what to do. Mrs. T____ found that Bobby couldn't read the second grade book, and that he stumbled with the words in a first grade book.

"Bobby's days in second grade varied from extreme emotional upset to somewhat calm days. He was not successfully motivated to read or to do his written assignments. If he discovered that academic work was difficult for him, he would become agitated and push it aside. He would also poke children next to him, scribble on their papers, and trip anyone who came near him. The other children began to dislike and avoid Bobby. This tended to make him even more hostile and irritable during the day.

"After Mrs. T____ described Bobby, I [the psychologist] asked if I could observe him in the classroom. On the day I visited, Bobby came into the room by banging the door and announcing loudly that he had arrived. This caused all the other children to groan loudly, and Bobby reacted by hitting the girl closest to him and making her cry. Mrs. T ____ , after gaining control of the situation, proceeded to start the day."

School Behavior and Reactions to Reading

Whatever the source, whether it be school psychologist, school social worker, teacher, or principal, if your child has reading problems, you should have more than a vague picture of his or her behavior in school. When teachers do not have the time or training for this, it is often most helpful to have a trained professional—a reading consultant, social worker or school psychologist—observe your child in class to get an objective and clear picture.

A child's emotional problems frequently interfere with his ability to learn to read. Just as frequently, a child's reading handicaps can result in various emotional problems. It is often extremely difficult to determine which problem is the cause and which is the result. When reading problems and emotional problems exist together, however, it is necessary that you become aware of both and attempt to deal with each in an appropriate way.

Children may react to reading disabilities by simply avoiding any activities that involve reading. The more parents and teachers demand work from such children, the more they tend to withdraw. We have seen high school boys and girls who read at a second grade level spending entire school days sitting in the back of the classroom, doing absolutely nothing. They will often prop a book up in front of them and hide behind it, hoping the teacher will not ask them any questions or expect any written work from them.

Frequently, the teacher will go along with such behavior knowing these pupils cannot do the work and are
beyond their help in the classroom. If they are quiet and
do not bother the teacher or other students, they may receive a passing grade, resulting in their moving on to the
next subject or the next grade—where the same process of
failure is repeated.

Other children may react aggressively to their own
lack of reading skills. At home, when a parent tries to per-
suade them to do their school work, they become hostile
and angry and react to the whole family in such an unpleasant manner that it soon becomes easier to ignore the whole
situation. In school, such children may become class
bullies. They may laugh at other children and taunt them
as they read or work at other school-related tasks. No matter how hard the teacher tries to help, they will usually re-
ject both the work and the teacher.

There are many other ways children develop negative
emotional responses to school work. Your child may have
experienced repeated failures at the beginning reading level,
and might even have suffered ridicule from other children
because of reading errors. The child could have developed
lack of confidence in other areas, which then extended
into his school work. Whatever may trigger them, negative
emotional responses can limit your child's ability to learn.

The school psychologist and/or school social worker, if properly trained, can provide advice to both teachers and parents on strategies that can reduce social and emotional causes of learning problems. Do not hesitate to seek such services from your school. Generally, professional staff members have so many requests and demands for their services that your child's problem may be deferred. It is your responsibility as a parent and a citizen to see that such assistance is available to you within a reasonable time after being requested.

Intelligence and Aptitude

Nearly all school psychologists, when a child is referred to them for learning problems, will attempt to determine the child's general intelligence or specific aptitudes for learning. Not all psychologists, however, hold the same view about what intelligence is, how it should be measured, what scores mean or what should be done.

There is an unfortunate amount of disagreement today, among lay people and professionals alike, over what "intelligence" tests measure. However, we should recognize that the crucial issue is how intelligence tests should be used, rather than whether or not they should be used at all. Intelligence tests can be used in ways known to be

actually harmful to children. If used properly, they can be
of considerable value to diagnostic and prescriptive work.
Administered and interpreted by trained persons, intelligence tests can be useful indicators of the general level of
a child's current functioning on various tasks of an academic sort.

Commonly used intelligence tests include measurements of a student's language and mathematical skills.
Among the skills tested, language tasks are usually the
most important because they are the most predictive of
general school performance.

However, we believe it to be a myth that general or
specialized tests of intelligence, aptitude, or achievement
can measure one's intellectual competence in all situations.
A person's problem solving skills shift from task to task.
We also believe that on any one given task, an individual's
performance can vary widely. People can become "smarter"
or less able, in the sense that they can become more or less
proficient in solving problems.

It is our duty as professional educators and it is your
obligation as parents to help children acquire those intellectual tools which, in a most real way, can help them become more efficient at solving their problems. Reading

skills are helpful, if not crucial, to being reasonably intelligent in this world. By helping your child to read better, you are making it possible for him or her to behave more intelligently today and tomorrow.

When your child has learned to read at a proficient level, you can have considerable confidence that he or she will be able to learn more easily. A poor showing on an intelligence test is no reason for placing a permanent score on any child's "intelligence." *Intelligence is not fixed.* It is the school's task and your task to help your child behave more intelligently. Your child's intelligence was not fixed for all time at the moment of conception. As important as heredity is, environment makes a big difference in how well any child performs. You can make your child "dumber" than he is today, or you can help to make him "brighter."

We believe that one's ability to solve problems through the use of the intellect can be modified, and our directions are simple.

1.   Avoid negative attitudes and punishments which can make your child insecure and so handicap his or her development.

2.   Learn to work effectively with teachers.

3.   Utilize experts for diagnosis of problem areas whenever possible.

4.   With the help of professional diagnosis and advice, practice methods of tutoring and encouraging reading that have been shown to have a likelihood of success.

THE READING SPECIALIST

Obtain the evaluations of a reading specialist. However, not every school provides a professionally trained reading specialist. Many teachers have had only one course in the teaching of reading. On the other hand, there are a great many teachers who are very competent.

Diagnostic Reading Services

The professional reading diagnostician usually has a minimum of a master's degree in reading and often has had a year or more of advanced work leading to a doctorate degree. Unfortunately, only the most enlightened and well financed schools have reading clinics with staffs of professional reading diagnosticians. If there is such a reading clinic within your school district and your child is not reading as you expect, your child should be referred to it.

In case your district has no reading clinic, there may be one at a nearby college or university. Reading clinics are frequently maintained by university and college learning centers for training teachers and reading specialists, for research on reading problems, and for tutorial services. These clinics are staffed by professionals who frequently work directly with severely disabled readers while supervising master's or doctoral level students in diagnostic and remedial techniques. Such clinics usually provide their services at little or no cost, depending upon family circumstances.

The Referral Process

Referrals to reading clinics can be made by teachers, principals, school psychologists, or parents. Before a reading specialist sees a child, considerable background information is needed to most effectively help a student.

The child's teacher will be asked to describe the student's overall behavior in relationship to the reading difficulty. The teacher will be asked to review the child's confidential record, to determine when reading problems were first noticed and the kinds of statements his or her former teachers might have made.

The reading specialist will also be concerned about whether or not your child reacted differently to different teachers. If the child had been evaluated by a school psychologist, a school social worker, or a child guidance clinic, the reading specialist will seek information from such sources. You will probably be asked to submit reports on the child's physical, visual, and hearing examinations and to fill out a medical statement.

In other words, all pertinent records, reports, and application forms must be made available to the reading specialist. Because most schools, private agencies, and doctors will not release any information about a child without your written permission, it will be up to you, the parent, to request records be sent to the reading clinic. You may feel that this is too much "red tape," but it is actually for the protection of both you and your child.

The Reading Examination Process

When all information is received, you will be notified of an appointment day. If a thorough examination is to be done, it usually takes most of a day. Your presence may also be required for most of the testing. In well equipped reading clinics, soundproof examining rooms are provided. Parents are often requested to observe, through one-way mirrors, the entire examination without their child being aware of parental surveillance. Through such observation, parents are often able to gain new insights into a youngster's reading problems.

Standardized Testing

The examiner will more than likely administer a standard diagnostic test such as the *Durrell Analysis of Reading Difficulty*. In order to administer this test, one must be specially trained. It is a long test, but it is very comprehensive and will give the examiner specific and needed information about an individual's reading abilities. The test measures: 1) reading level, 2) speed of reading, 3) types of errors made, 4) comprehension, 5) rate of silent reading, 6) understanding of silent reading, 7) grade level of word recognition, 8) speed of word recognition, 9) letter names and sounds, 10) blend and digraph sounds, 11) spelling skills, and 12) memory for new words taught.

The examiner may also administer group or other individual achievement tests to determine how the scores on one might compare with the scores on the other. A good examiner will seldom rely on one test for a diagnosis.

The examiner will also have a series of reading textbooks so that an "informal reading test" can be administered. On this test, the examiner merely opens a textbook to a page at random and asks the child to read. Two or three books may be used, each written at different grade levels, to determine at what level the child can read quickly, accurately, and comfortably.

LEARNING DISABILITIES

There are few phrases in education which are more misunderstood than the phrase "learning disabilities." Many different definitions of learning disability have been offered by educators, thus contributing to the confusion. However, all of the definitions recognize one basic condition: there are students "with a problem in understanding or in using spoken or written language."* As further stated in a publication of the Association for Children with

---

Specific Learning Disabilities . . . A First Look for Parents, published by Kiwanis International in cooperation with the Association for Children with Learning Disabilities, 1975.

Learning Disabilities: "Some disabilities are referred to as 'specific' learning disabilities . . . to differentiate them from other disabilities, which are primarily due to mental retardation, emotional disturbance, poor vision or poor hearing, or cultural disadvantage. The child with a specific learning disability is of average or above intellect."*

Among the more commonly discussed types of "specific learning disabilities" is dyslexia, which some assume to be a type of minimal brain disfunction. Others prefer the terms, "perceptual handicap" or "neurological handicap." In any event, as a tutor you will face these terms and perhaps the conditions to which they refer.

Dyslexia

Dyslexia has been defined as "inability to learn to read, or word blindness." It must be stressed here that this is a very difficult condition for even the most competent experts to diagnose. In fact, authorities themselves have not yet agreed upon what actually constitutes dyslexia. What they do agree upon is that, in spite of years of very

---

*Ibid.

intensive remedial instruction in reading by specialists, some children do not learn to read very well. When such children do learn to read even at a very low level, their reading is a slow and painful process. Some specialists feel that such reading difficulties are caused by a brain injury. Brain injury is usually discovered through an EEG test (electroencephalogram), which is used to determine brain wave patterns. It must be emphasized that most children with reading problems are quite normal as far as brain wave patterns are concerned.

Unfortunately, there have been parents who were relieved when their child was diagnosed as "dyslexic." They may have felt that, since this indicates a possible congenital condition, they are relieved of any blame for their child's reading problem and so have no responsibility to help overcome the impairment. This is one reason why we have always hesitated to pin this label on a child.

No matter what the case, we would seldom give up on helping a child to learn to read better.

Here are some characteristics commonly associated with dyslexia. The child:

1. is frequently confused about time, distance, direction, and size;

2. often has difficulty discriminating between sounds and does not seem to hear certain sounds —thus has difficulty learning to reproduce them correctly;

3. has trouble telling right from left;

4. cannot seem to remember words even after they have been taught repeatedly and even after being instructed as to their sounds, forms and meanings. Prompted on a word in one line, the child may not remember the same word in the next line.

The best technique to use with a dyslexic child (as with any child with a reading disability) is to begin at a very low level, where he or she can continually experience success even though moving at a "snail's pace." The instructor must make sure that the student has thoroughly mastered a skill before proceeding to another level.

For example, if you want your child to learn the consonant sound "b," stick with the sound until it is recognized every single time it is seen. This will mean much review of material taught, but it will be worth the effort.

Always bear in mind that you will have to be satisfied with small successes in the beginning. If you try to teach too much at one time, you will only confuse and frustrate your child to the point that all will be lost.

Going through the diagnosis provided in this book may help you to understand what the exact reading problem is. If your child happens to fit many of the categories of dyslexia, don't despair; you will simply have to work a little harder, go at a slower pace, and repeat frequently what you are absolutely sure was mastered (only to discover that it may be "forgotten" again and again).

If you find that your child is unable to tell time or to determine distance, direction, and size, it will be wise to bring these concepts into focus, not necessarily just at reading time, but as frequently as possible. If you are fully aware that the condition exists, you will understand that your child is not be be blamed for failure to learn what has been seemingly taught.

Some children learn reading concepts quite readily and almost incidentally, but others do not. Consider for example the following case of Patty:

Patty is an attractive, alert sixth grade student. During her first year of school, she had been successful at learning to read. Her second grade experience was quite unfortunate, and she did not gain a year in reading. Her teacher had been cold and punitive, and Patty had become fearful of failure; she refused to attempt to read. Consequently, when she entered third grade, still reading at a first grade level, she was sent to the remedial reading teacher. That specialist described her as "highly distractible and lacking in interest in learning to read." The teacher noted Patty had quickly learned the technique of avoidance by having other students do the assigned classroom work for her.

When she was in fourth grade, her mother, Mrs. S___ , enrolled Patty in a private reading clinic. There she was diagnosed as having dyslexia, and she left school during part of each day for an entire year to attend this clinic. During the other part of the day, she was seen by the school remedial reading teacher and received help from her regular classroom teacher.

At the end of the school year, Patty was dismissed from the clinic because the teachers felt they could not help her; she was now reading at a second grade level.

Mrs. S____ had informed the clinic that Patty's father had a severe reading problem, and that even as an adult, he was a virtual non-reader. She said her husband was employed in a job that required little reading and that she helped him when necessary. As a result, the clinic personnel diagnosed Patty's reading problem as partly family related and suggested to Mrs. S____ that she help Patty accept her reading problem and not "feel badly" about it.

As a result, Patty began freely to tell people she "couldn't read" and completely avoided trying. Unfortunately, Patty's teachers did not agree that she was unable to learn reading, and they expected the same assignments from her as they did from the other students. All of Patty's "good" friends continued to do her work for her, and her achievement level dropped even lower than it was when she was in fourth grade.

Did this defeatist attitude help Patty? Who can say for sure that the girl's reading problem is *en famille*? We are unwilling to accept such a claim; but even if it were true, we could not justify either shrugging it off or stressing it as an "unchangeable" condition.

When we began working on this case, we aggressively encouraged both the child and her mother to gain confidence in Patty's individual abilities. Then, using a systematic, step-by-step process, we sorted out which skills the child already possessed for reading and which ones she lacked. This enabled us to work up a program for Patty's mother to follow with her. As a result, the child began to show real progress, which stimulated her to greater effort and also reassured her mother. At present, there is every indication that Patty will gradually raise her reading ability to a satisfactory level.

Lateral Dominance

A number of educators have considered the implications of lateral dominance in attempting to explain some types of reading disability. Lateral dominance refers to which side of the body (left or right) is dominant over the other.

Is the child left handed or right handed? Is the left eye dominant over the right eye? It has been noted that some children who have not established dominance (who use right or left hand interchangeably) and some who have crossed dominance (right eyed, left handed), also have difficulty learning to read. However, there is considerable disagreement as to whether or not the lack of dominance can be considered as a cause of reading problems.

There was a time when children who preferred to use their left hands were forced to change and learn to use their right hands. This frequently produced mixed dominance, with children growing up using both hands. Some authorities have suggested this practice of training left handed persons to be right handed as a cause of reading problems; however, this view has been pretty much discarded by most experts.

Even so, many people still believe that lateral dominance is a cause of reading failure. We know that large numbers of children learn to read with no difficulty, even though they are left handed and right eyed.

Since there is disagreement and the data are inconclusive, we would certainly suggest that you be open-minded about what future research will conclude. In any event, if your child lacks lateral dominance, he or she can be helped to read better. We have found the lack of lateral dominance to be no great barrier in teaching reading skills to formerly poor readers.

Motivation

The reading specialist will also attempt to make an assessment of the presence of certain motivational conditions. One personal condition of extreme importance is whether your child believes that he or she is capable of learning to read well. For most poor readers, the number one handicap they must overcome is a low self-concept of academic ability; this is almost invariably the result of having been criticized and stigmatized for failure.

The reading specialist in such a case will instruct you how to be effective in helping your youngster to acquire self-confidence.

You, also, may need confidence; for many parents unknowingly communicate this attitude to their children. In the last chapter of this book, we will offer you some specific guidelines to follow for the enhancement and maintenance of adequate and healthy self-assurance of academic ability.

TEACHER EFFECTIVENESS

We hesitate to include ineffective teaching as a possible cause of reading failure because it is often used as an

easy excuse. However, occasionally we have seen classrooms in which necessary reading skills are poorly taught.
In some classrooms, we have seen large proportions of
children fail to learn year after year simply because of
inept teaching.

At the other extreme, there are those classrooms in
which nearly every child, regardless of social class, race,
sex, or physical characteristics, learns to read at a level in
advance of his or her age. This is too much to expect of all
teachers given the conditions under which most must teach.
Fortunately, the majority of teachers do a very good job
with most students in spite of the many impediments they
must overcome.

We have also seen teachers who are relatively successful at teaching reading skills, but who do not encourage
student interests in reading. We recognize the value of not
only being able to read, but also of being interested in
reading. It is important to realize that both reading skill
and interest in reading are learned and that both must be
promoted.

We have observed classrooms where reading becomes
something to associate with pain. For example, in some
well disciplined classrooms, each child may be required to
take his or her turn standing and reading aloud. This can

prove to be extremely embarrassing for the child who is off to a slow start, and such a child may quickly develop an intense dislike for reading. Fortunately, this type of teaching is becoming increasingly rare; nonetheless, it still exists.

There is also an occasional teacher who makes learning to read so boring that a child may lose interest at the very beginning. For example, a teacher may feel that children must learn all of the letter names and sounds before they are given books to read. All available reading instruction time is spent in drilling the children over and over on letter sounds until every child has mastered them. Drill can be an effective part of the teaching of reading, but this method alone is usually extremely tiresome and frustrating to students.

A word of caution at this point: under no circumstances should you openly criticize the teacher regarding his or her method of teaching reading. If you do, you may feel better for making your views known, but you may well harm your child's interests. You may find that the teacher's willingness to cooperate with you in your attempt to help your child has quickly diminished. Teachers usually feel that they are doing their best, and they like to think that their methods of teaching reading are the most effective.

Also, keep in mind that teachers are often under a great deal of pressure. These days, they are constantly being evaluated in terms of how well they cover a rather broad curriculum. Teachers who are responsible for mathematics, reading, science, spelling, English, social studies, art, music, library time, field trips, milk money collection, physical education (and any other special subject that may come along) find that their days are filled to capacity. Thus, it should be understandable when a teacher has relatively little time to devote to an individual child who has fallen behind in reading.

In any case, there is much more to be gained from eliciting cooperation than from incurring resentment. If you are aware of certain inadequacies in your child's classroom instruction, try to compensate through your own efforts. After you have completely read this book and discussed your child's situation with a reading specialist, you will know better how to proceed. Let the reading specialist develop the important conclusions.

After the examiner has administered all of the standard and specialized examinations, you may be invited to a conference with the examiner so that you can go over the day's testing. If you have been able to view the testing, you will probably be quite enlightened about your child's reading difficulty even before you see the test results.

All of the results will be written in report form. Specific recommendations will be made for the correction of each specific reading problem. Copies should be made available to you for distribution to your child's teacher, counselor, and/or remedial reading teacher.

You should go over the report with your child's teachers so that you can gain an understanding of their methods for implementing the recommendations that have been made.

3

The Home Environment

Certain points in this chapter may arouse negative reactions in you as a parent. Our aim is not to put you on the defensive or to make you feel guilty concerning past mistakes. Everybody makes mistakes—usually without being aware of them. However, recognition of our mistakes can enable us to correct them.

To provide a setting favorable to helping your child, you may need first to face some difficult questions and then to deal with them in a constructive manner. The important thing is: don't dwell on past mistakes; rather, begin positive action at once.

The recommendations in this chapter are based on techniques that have proved effective in successful parent-child relationships. Putting them into practice will help you establish a comfortable—and practical—background for helping your child. Topics to be discussed are:

- Important Questions to Consider

- Deciding Which Parent Should Tutor

- Choosing the Right Time and Place

- What to Tell Other Family Members

- Getting Started

- Developing Good Tutoring Habits

- The Importance of Diet and Rest

IMPORTANT QUESTIONS TO CONSIDER

"Have I contributed to my child's reading problems?"
This is a question many parents ask and it is deserving of
an answer. Admittedly, reading problems have various and
complex causes, quite apart from anything a parent may or
may not do, but it might be wise to begin by asking yourself the following questions and to be very honest in an-
swering them.

1. Am I overly anxious about my child's reading? Do I pressure the child constantly to do better?

2. Do I openly compare this child unfavorably with other children in the family? (There are many times when a younger sister or brother is able to read circles around an older sibling. The younger children may make such comparisons; however, parents should be quick to mention the child's more positive features, rather than contribute to his or her discouragement.)

3. Does my child go to school in a cheerful mood?

4. Do I tend to blame others for my child's inability to read?

5. Is my child healthy, well rested, and properly nourished each day?

6. Does my child regularly talk to me at length about school and other interests?

DECIDING WHICH PARENT SHOULD TUTOR

Designate one parent to conduct all of the reading sessions. In our society, it is often the mother who tries to help the children learn reading. However, many fathers should also be involved in helping their children to overcome poor reading habits. In your case, you should jointly decide which parent will work with the child on a regular basis each day. The decision should be based on mutual agreement as to which one is the more able—not which one has the time. Once you and your spouse decide who is to meet in scheduled activity with the child, plans can be made for ways the other parent can also help.

Both parents, if possible, should study this book; but for consistency, only one should conduct the regular afternoon or evening sessions. Perhaps after five or six weeks, you will wish to try an exchange of duties. However, if the child is progressing you will probably wish to continue with the original arrangements.

You should not change session leaders at the first sign of frustration. In some cases it may take several weeks to discern major improvements in reading skills—so don't expect too much at first.

Also, parents must make it a rule never to disagree in the child's presence about the approach to reading. The parent who is meeting with the child regularly needs full cooperative support from the other parent.

CHOOSING THE RIGHT TIME AND PLACE

It is not an easy task for parents to do all that needs to be done for their children. Parents of children who are experiencing reading problems may believe they do not have the needed facilities, professional training, or time to give proper help. We have often heard comments such as: "It is so hard for me to work with my child. We live in a small house and the kitchen table is often used by the other children in the family"; "The television is going all the time"; "Our boys share rooms"; and "My husband and I are both too busy just trying to make ends meet."

These commonly cited problems, encountered by many parents who have talked to us about reading difficulties, only emphasize the necessity for a well organized plan of attack on the problem.

Selecting a Study Area

The number of rooms in your house is of little importance. You can help your child be a better reader in an extremely limited amount of space; but it may take some forethought and planning.

Start by deciding on a regular place to work. Since all of the other rooms are usually in use, you might use your own bedroom. This is frequently the one room in the house that is not in the main line of family activity. You don't have to have a desk; the bed will work fine.

At the very first session, be equipped with paper, pencils, crayons, pictorially described stories and perhaps a small bag of candy or cookies to share with your child.

When to Tutor

No time will be perfect for you, since you have many other responsibilities and not all of them are regularly scheduled. However, if you are going to help your child on a planned basis, your study sessions should be definitely scheduled and given as much importance as any other time commitment in your life.

Select the best time for you and your child to meet regularly, four or five sessions a week. Try to leave weekends free. Remember, once you have selected a time, stick to it without exception—barring emergencies of course.

It will be much easier on everyone when this activity becomes a part of the regular daily schedule. We have found 7 p.m. to be a good time, since dinner is usually over by then and the news occupies the television. If Mother is the tutor, she should be more compulsive about helping a child than about getting the dishes washed right away. If Father is the tutor, he can usually manage to learn about what appeared on the newscast a bit later.

In any event, try to select a time that will be least troublesome to your child. For best results, it should be early in the evening or else during late afternoon, if possible.

WHAT TO TELL OTHER FAMILY MEMBERS

After you have found a time and place to work, you need to explain to the rest of the family what is going on. Have a talk with the other children before you start your

reading program so that they will understand the importance of what you are doing. Emphasize that success will
substantially depend upon cooperation from each member
of the family.

When the chosen time comes around, drop whatever
you are doing, take your child into your room and close
the door. Ask the others not to disturb you unless there is
a real emergency. Siblings may be curious and want to
watch, but for obvious reasons, it is better to insist on pri-
vacy.

When the session is over, answer any questions from
the family with optimistic comments on your child's progress. Always find something to praise in the child's performance; and be sure to voice your praise in the child's
presence. (If you should feel discouraged, keep it to yourself—again for obvious reasons.)

GETTING STARTED

You may want to spend the first session just talking
with your youngster about his or her reading problem. Ask
the child to help you decide what should be worked on

first. Try to make it a pleasant and relaxing time so that the youngster will look forward to your next meeting.

If you are consistent, pleasant, and positive with your child at all times, you are sure to succeed in your efforts to help him or her make improvement in reading skills. However, be prepared to be patient; it sometimes takes time before progress becomes apparent.

You might also find that you will get to know your child better in the process of tutoring. Busy parents often find little opportunity to have serious conversations for more than a few minutes with their children at any one time. These sessions can help you to become aware of his or her thoughts and feelings about school; of attitudes about school and the family; and reasons for previously misunderstood behavior.

Keep the sessions very loosely structured in the beginning; building a comfortable, cordial relationship is the most important consideration at first. Later, the sessions can take on more structure, but they should never become so rigid that the child loses interest.

The amount of time you should spend in a session will naturally depend upon individual judgment. If you feel that after five minutes your child is becoming restless, frustrated, or tired of it all, then that is definitely the time to quit. The chances are that forcing him or her to work after such symptoms appear will serve no useful purpose. If you are relaxed in your approach, the days that you can work only five minutes will gradually give way to other days when you will be able to get in an hour.

If the child is restless, frustrated or bored, you will have to work on that problem before you can assess or teach reading effectively. Unfortunately, some parents too easily become impatient with their children; but if you show interest in the material, the child's interest will be aroused. Usually, the sessions can be built upon a series of activities which are interesting to you both. Suggestions for such activities are given in later chapters.

DEVELOPING GOOD TUTORING HABITS

The following typical statement describes the quandry of many parents when they realize that their child's reading disability has begun to affect his or her performance in all areas of school work:

> "I know my Billy has assignments, but he
> never brings them home. When he does bring his

books home, he hides them in the closet and
then I see him taking them back to school the
next day. I know he can't read the books, but he
doesn't seem to want me to help him."

The need for action is obvious. For the child's sake,
the parent should take charge of setting up systematic help
sessions. Good tutoring habits will guide the development
of effective study habits.

Contact the School

Begin by calling your youngster's teacher (or teachers)
requesting a special conference. Ask whether or not your
child has been handing in homework. The teacher will
probably show you the record book and you can see for
yourself how few or many assignments your child has completed.

Be in Regular Communication

If it turns out that your child has been failing to turn
in homework assignments, it may be necessary to set up
some regular communication with the teacher, so that you
will know when the child has homework to do. Have the

teacher give you a call, if possible. (This is often difficult
for teachers to do, since their time is taken up with many
activities; but such communication will be in the interests
of the teacher, as well as of you and your child.)

One thing you will soon discover is that even if the
teacher has attempted to provide materials for your child
at his or her reading level, the assignments may still be far
too difficult for the youngster to attempt. It is sometimes
easier for a poor reader to ignore the whole thing than to
make an effort that is likely to end in failure. Further preparation for parent-teacher conferences is described in
Chapter 4.

Homework

Once you have learned what the assignments are, go
over the work your child brings home, step-by-step. While
you should not provide answers or do the child's work,
you may find it necessary to give help with almost every
word the student must read or write; but do so—and get it
out of the way, so you can proceed with meaningful reading instruction. Do not be punitive or critical; poor readers
do not feel any better about their failures than their parents do. They do, however, need to develop the habit of
doing all work expected of them by their teachers, even if
it isn't perfect. This habit can be learned only if parents

keep track of assignments, work the lessons out carefully with such children, and make sure their homework is handed in on time.

Sometimes reading skills improve merely by establishing good work habits; this may be all that is needed to break the vicious circle that has developed as a child gets farther and farther behind in assignments.

Avoid Emotionally-loaded Pressure

You must be careful not to use too much pressure in getting your child to complete assignments. If the child is made to feel guilty, threatened or forced into doing homework, your purpose of helpfulness may be defeated. The correct approach is to give the child an abundance of praise for any small accomplishment.

Never criticize, no matter how much you may feel like doing so at times. Approach each lesson in a cheerful manner; let your child know you are confident he or she can succeed in reading; and if you can't praise for successes at first, use comments such as "That was a hard word (or sentence), wasn't it?" or "I'm proud of you for making such a good try."

First of all, accept your child's reading disability in a matter-of-fact way. To let the child believe you consider him or her a failure and a disappointment will serve no useful purpose; it may be harmful.

This doesn't mean that you have to be dishonest. After you have thoroughly studied this book and discussed the procedures to be followed with the support of your spouse, talk to the youngster as you would to another adult. Inform the child that you have contacted his or her teacher and other specialists discussed in Chapter 2. Mention frankly that you have found out what is causing the reading problem, and what course of action you are going to follow. But do it in a casual way. You may be surprised at how well your child will respond to this direct, honest approach.

Make Rules for Yourself

Before you begin any type of program to help your child, you must first make a set of rules—not for the child, but for yourself. We cannot stress the importance of this too much. Should you repeatedly become frustrated and anxious and feel like spanking the youngster for not remembering, you might as well throw this book away and forget trying to be of help.

Rules for yourself should cover such things as keeping a regular schedule, constantly considering the child's point of view, controlling your own frustrations, and remembering to praise even the child's most minor accomplishments while ignoring his or her failures. Such tactics may seem difficult to learn, but they become easier to practice as results prove their value.

THE IMPORTANCE OF DIET

Children who do not eat breakfast often become tired and hungry before lunch. Some youngsters fill up on foods that are deficient in necessary nutrients and vitamins. Unfortunately, malnutrition is characteristic of many children in our society and occurs at all income levels. There are generally two reasons for this: poverty, and/or parental unawareness of what constitutes a healthy diet.

Don't take it for granted that you know what a proper diet is, or that your child is receiving all of the right foods. Consult a nurse, doctor, or dietitian; obtain a book on nutrition. Then compare what your child has been eating with the experts' suggestions. It will give you confidence if you find that, for a fact, your child has been getting the proper nourishment. If you discover dietary deficiencies, you will know exactly what to do to improve your child's eating habits and health.

THE IMPORTANCE OF REST

Make sure your child has plenty of rest. Perhaps no other problem is so difficult to deal with as is the simple matter of getting too little sleep. Children who stay up much too late at night watching television usually have a difficult time the next day. There are children who fall asleep during the afternoon or may be so sluggish and inattentive that little learning takes place.

SUMMARY

This chapter has dealt with basic procedures for providing a home environment that is conducive to successful tutoring by parents. The main points considered involve preparation for, and getting started in, a program to help your child.

Elements that have proved to contribute to effective tutoring were discussed, beginning with an examination of parental attitudes, under the heading "Important Questions to Consider."

You have been advised to:

1. Avoid anxiety and negative statements concerning your child's reading problem;

2. Make one parent responsible for conducting actual tutoring;

3. Select an appropriate time and place for regular sessions;

4. Keep sessions private; also praise your child's progress in the presence of other family members;

5. Ease into structured sessions by starting gradually while showing your child your eagerness to help;

6. Develop good tutoring habits by making rules for yourself; and

7.   Make sure your child is getting an adequate diet and sufficient rest.

In the next section on assessment, we provide you with a number of specific questions that may facilitate better communication between you and your child's teacher. Remember, the teacher will probably have a vested interest in your help. Most teachers need and want full communication with parents. For your child's sake, make it a regular habit to build bridges between home and school.

4

Parent Teacher Conferences

In this and the following chapter you will learn to determine which particular skills and attitudes your child needs help with and where to begin.

Following a parent-teacher conference (which is the first essential step), you will need to know the following procedures:

- How to determine the levels at which your child can read both orally and silently;

- How to find out whether or not your youngster understands what is being read;

- How to measure the child's knowledge of letter-sounds;

- How to discover whether or not your child can discriminate between similar sounds; and

- How to discover the levels at which your child is
  able to recognize words quickly and accurately
  without having to stop to study each word carefully.

TALK TO YOUR CHILD'S TEACHER

Too often parents leave teacher conferences without
having gained much practical information. Asking the right
questions will increase your chances of gaining an understanding of the nature of your child's reading difficulties.

The first thing to remember is the importance of
friendly communication with the teacher. Almost any
teacher appreciates support and interest from parents and
will cooperate with your desire to help improve your child's
reading skills. Also, a student who knows that the home
and school are working together will tend to respond posi-
tively to your attention.

QUESTIONS TO ASK

Following is a list of suggested questions you might ask a teacher. The list is by no means complete for each individual child. Since you know your own child, you will no doubt have other questions which need answers; however, these can help you get started.

1. What is my child's reading level?

2. May I see the results of my child's latest standardized reading test?* (These results are usually available to parents if they ask. You should, however, ask the teacher to interpret them for you, as meanings of scores may differ from test-to-test, and even on different parts of the same test.)

---

*Standardized reading or achievement tests are published commercially and used nationwide. The results compare one individual child with hundreds of other children of the same age and grade placement. The *Metropolitan Achievement Test*, the *Stanford Achievement Test*, and the *California Achievement Test* are some of the more popular tests administered in school systems.

3. Does my child

    a. read voluntarily?

    b. appear to like reading?

    c. listen carefully in a group?

    d. pay attention to directions?

    e. tire easily?

    f. become easily upset?

    g. get along with other children at school? (If the answer is "no," try to find out why.)

4. In addition, you might ask,

    a. How do other children react to my child?

    b. Do you feel he or she is putting forth maximum effort at school?

    c. And (most important of all), What do you feel is the cause of my child's reading problem?

After you have asked questions such as these, you will leave the parent-teacher conference with a better understanding of your child's school experiences. The information you gain will also help you in preparing to help your child.

PART B

FINDING A STARTING POINT

5

Assessing Reading Skills

Before you begin working with your child, there are simple tests you can use to determine his or her present reading levels in oral and silent reading. Knowing these levels will enable you to avoid starting your program with material that is either too difficult or too easy. We will begin with descriptions of the three levels of oral reading, and simple instructions for determining them.

THREE LEVELS OF READING

Frustrational Level

This is the level at which many words become barriers to reading. It measures the point at which a child gives up because the material is too difficult. A teacher or parent may inadvertently try to teach words that are more frustration-producing than instructional. When too many unfamiliar words become barriers to general understanding, children tend to develop a dislike for reading. Your double objective should be to help your child to read better and to make reading an enjoyable activity.

Instructional Level

This is the level at which you should teach reading. At this level your child will be learning new words, as well as learning how to figure out unknown words.

Independent Level

The independent level is the level at which one can read quickly and easily without aid. For example, suppose a student in the fourth grade becomes resentful and frustrated with reading fourth grade level reading materials, even though able to read and understand many words. This child may find third grade material much easier; he or she won't miss quite so many words on a page at this level, and with help, will be able to figure out all of the new words. In this case, third grade material would be the instructional level. If the same child is able to pick up a second grade book and read it quickly and feel comfortable with it, second grade materials are at his or her independent level.

MEASURING ORAL READING LEVELS

If you wish to determine your child's reading skills according to the three different levels, the easiest way is to give him or her paragraphs to read from several grade levels. In Appendix A you will find paragraphs copied from reading books used in grade levels primer through four.

Directions

1. Appendix A contains the reading material to be handed to your child when oral reading measurements begin.

2. This is important! As your child reads the stories in Appendix A, record mistakes on a separate sheet of paper. For example, if your youngster says *saw* for *was*, write "saw - was." Recording reading errors will provide knowledge of the kinds of mistakes your child makes at each level and give you clues for offering help at the proper instructional level.

3. After your child has read each paragraph, ask the series of comprehension questions that follow. This will determine if your child understands what he or she has

just read. For your convenience, correct answers to all questions are supplied so that you can easily mark on a separate sheet of paper each correct or wrong response.

4.   When wrong responses appear to be completely unrelated to what has been read, it is advisable to write down the incorrect answer. This furnishes a complete record for you to study later and will help you learn more about how your child's mind functions.

Comprehension Questions: Oral Reading Skills

For Appendix A - Primer Level:

1.   Who did Peter go to see? _____
      (a wise old man)

2.   What made noise? _____
      (house, bed, door, window)

3.   Why would Peter be concerned about the noise?

      _____

      (he wanted to go to sleep)

For Appendix A - Level 1:

1. Where had Bobby gone? _____
    (down the street)

2. What did he have to tell his friends?

    _____

    (good-by)

3. What did he give away? _____
    (goldfish, turtle, frog)

4. Why do you suppose he was giving everything
    away? _____
    (he was moving)

For Appendix A - Level 2:

1. Where were Tammy and her family?

    _____

    (in the Rocky Mountains)

2. What was her family doing in the mountains?

    _____

    (camping)

3. What did Ann have with her? _____
    (a camera)

4. What did Dad have that Ann wanted to show in
    the picture? _____
    (the pack)

For Appendix A - Level 3:

   1.   Who is the main character in the story?

       _____

       (the Old Lady)

   2.   Where did she live? _____
       (on top of a hill)

   3.   Who lived with the Old Lady?

       _____

       (her animal friends—a Brindle Cat, a Magic
       Mouse, and an alligator named Alexander)

For Appendix A - Level 4:

1. Who is the story about? _____
    (Louis Armstrong)

2. Where was he born? _____
    (New Orleans)

3. What instrument did he play? _____
    (trumpet)

4. Why is he considered one of the greatest jazz
    musicians? _____
    (introduced jazz as an art form around the world)

Summary of Oral Reading Skills

After your child has responded to the above questions, you may want to excuse him or her for three to five minutes to get a drink or something. Take a few minutes yourself and review your child's responses and answer on a separate sheet of paper the following questions:

1. Comprehension (number of questions missed)

    a. Primer paragraph _____

    b. First grade paragraph _____

    c. Second grade paragraph _____

    d. Third grade paragraph _____

    e. Fourth grade paragraph _____

2. Indicate your assessment of your child's reading level.

    a. Independent _____
        (level which child reads and comprehends all material easily)

b.   Instructional _____
(level which child understands, but has difficulty with some words)

c.   Frustrational _____
(level which child finds too difficult to read or understand)

3.   If you can, answer yes or no.

Did your child:

a.   reverse words (saw for was, you for boy, etc.)?
_____

b.   look at words quickly and then guess at them (when for then, what for where, him for his, etc.)? _____

c.   add words while reading? _____

d.   omit words? _____

e.   point to each word while reading? _____

f.   forget a word from one line to the next?
_____

g. read quickly and smoothly without pausing to sound out each word as it was read? _____

h. make mistakes on easy words and remember the harder ones? _____

i. make self-corrections while reading? _____

j. make sense out of the material? _____

k. read voluntarily? _____

COMPREHENSION WHILE SILENT READING

There are many children who read aloud quite well, but when they are asked to read "to themselves," they are unable to do so. This is frequently caused by a method of early instruction in which a teacher begins by having children read aloud, but neglects teaching them to read to themselves. In this situation, children sometimes learn "words" without developing an understanding of what they are reading.

There are other children who do very well when reading silently. They are able to read a story to themselves and determine its entire meaning. A simple test to determine the level of your child's silent reading is presented below for use with Appendix B, at the same levels and order as the oral check-tests explained in the preceding section. Appendix B is for your child to read.

Directions

Since you have determined your child's independent oral reading level, when you begin silent reading measurements you can start him or her at that level. For example, if your child's oral independent level is at Level 2, ask your

child to read Level 2 in Appendix B silently. If all comprehension questions are answered correctly, and if questions
are missed at Level 3, you will know that Level 2 is your
child's silent independent reading level. However, if questions are missed at Level 2, proceed *downward* to determine his or her silent independent reading level.

Comprehension Questions: Silent Reading Skills

For Appendix B - Primer Level:

1. Who was the story about? _____
    (Mike)

2. What was in the tree? _____
    (a bird)

3. What color was the bird? _____
    (blue)

For Appendix B - Level 1:

1. Who is the story about? _____
    (a rabbit)

2. Who does the rabbit live with? _____
    (his mother)

3. What did the rabbit need to make him happy?

    _____

    (friends to play with)

4. What did the rabbit want his mother to do?

    _____

    (tell him a story about a brave little rabbit)

For Appendix B - Level 2:

1. What was the man's name? _____
    (Rambling Richard)

2. Why do you suppose he was called Rambling
    Richard? _____
    (he liked to go from town to town)

3. What did he like to do every day?

    _____

    (write a story)

4. What kind of stories did he like to write?

    _____

    (real, make-believe, funny, or sad)

For Appendix B - Level 3:

1. What was the story about? _____
    (fishing)

2. How did men catch fish thousands of years ago?

    _____

    (with their hands, tossed spears at them, or shot
    them with bows and arrows)

3. Do the fishermen catch enough fish to feed the
    people now? _____
    (no)

4. Where must we go to buy more fish? _____
    (other countries)

For Appendix B - Level 4:

1.   What does the word "dinosaur" mean?

     _____

     (terrible lizard)

2.   What animals belong to the same reptile family
     today? _____
     (lizards, snakes, crocodiles)

3.   How heavy were the dinosaurs as compared with
     the elephants? _____
     (heavier than a dozen elephants)

4.   How did some dinosaurs walk? _____
     (on their hind legs)

Summary of Silent Reading Skills

1. At what level did your child read quickly and understand what was read? _____

2. Did your youngster whisper while reading?

    _____

3. Did your youngster ask you to pronounce any of the words? _____
    If so, how many? _____

MEASURING
AUDITORY DISCRIMINATION SKILLS

Auditory discrimination means hearing differences between sounds. It is surprising how many children do not hear the sounds correctly and cannot tell one sound from another. Techniques for correcting this are discussed in Chapter 7.

This is a listening test for the child so you will be doing the reading. By marking any wrong responses your child may make, you will get a record of sounds your child has difficulty in distinguishing. This record will be of use when you begin regular help-sessions with your child.

Directions

1.   Copy the following word sets on a separate sheet of paper.

2.   Seat your youngster in a chair facing a wall. Using the following word sets, stand behind him or her, and in a normal tone of voice say:

> "I am going to say three words. Two
> words are alike and one is different.
> Tell me which word is different."

3.   Draw a circle around each wrong response on your copy of the following word sets.

4.   Answer on a separate sheet of paper the questions following the word sets.

Word Sets

1.	about	2.	what	3.	bound
	above		when		bought
	about		what		bound

4.	came	5.	street	6.	book
	came		stripe		look
	come		stripe		book

7.	cat	8.	been	9.	bark
	can		been		back
	can		bean		bark

10.	bring	11.	away	12.	slay
	ring		awake		slay
	ring		away		play

Summary of Auditory Discrimination Skills

1. Did your youngster:

    a. distinguish between sounds when words
        were similar? _____

    b. hear beginning sounds? _____

    c. hear ending sounds? _____

    d. hear middle sounds? _____

2. Which sounds were troublesome? _____

MEASURING PHONETIC SKILLS

The phonics approach to teaching reading has been a controversial subject for many years. Many educational battles have been fought over whether a child should be taught by the phonic method or the sight (look-say) method. Our position is that both methods need and should be taught.

The word phonic merely means "producing sounds." In the case of reading, it means producing the sounds for each of the letters in the alphabet. A child needs to develop this skill in order to learn to identify words without constant help.

Some teachers drill their students over the sounds of individual letters, from "A" to "Z." Others teach phonetics by having the children listen carefully for beginning sounds. For example, a routine such as this might be followed: "a" - apple, "b" - ball, "c" - cat, "d" - dog, continuing through words beginning with "z." Children will then be asked to name words they can think of that begin *like* apple, ball, cat, dog, and so on through the alphabet. Thus, children are taught to listen closely to sounds, and to associate them with other words in their vocabularies.

Consonants and Vowels

Normally, children learn phonetics in first grade. There are many cases, however, in which a child is not ready to master letter sounds at this level. In the next part of the diagnosis you can determine whether or not your child knows letter sounds thoroughly. The materials are divided into two parts, consonants and vowels. (Consonants are the letters b, c, d, f, g, h, j, k, l, m, n, p, q, r, s, t, v, w, x, y, and z; and vowels are a, e, i, o, and u.) Frequently, children easily master consonant sounds but have trouble with vowels. This is due to the fact that vowels have more than one sound, occur in the middle of words, or can be "silent" in a word, so it is difficult to attach the correct sounds to them in different combinations of spelling.

Directions: Consonant and Vowel Sounds

1.   In Appendix C you will find the consonant and vowel sounds. Hand Appendix C to your youngster. Point to the consonant letters and say: "Tell me the sound that each of these letters makes."

b   c   d   f   g   h   j

k   l   m   n   p   q   r

s   t   v   w   x   y   z

2.   As your child reads the sound of each letter, record the wrong responses on a separate sheet of paper. This will tell you which consonants your child needs to work on.

3.   Now point to the vowel letters, saying, "Tell me the sound that each of these letters makes."

a   e   i   o   u

4.   Repeat the procedure for recording wrong responses. Letters missed will tell you which vowels your child needs to work on. If your child does not pronounce both "long and short" sounds, go back over the letters to find out whether or not all basic vowel sounds have been learned.

Digraphs and Blends

The next part of the diagnosis of phonic skills will be to determine if your child knows the digraph and blend sounds.

Digraphs are two consonant letters which combine to make one sound. Examples of digraphs are: *sh* as in shoe, short, shop, shout, should; *th* as in thank, that, these, those, this; *wh* as in what, which, why, where; *ch* as in chance, chop, cheese, choose.

Blends are two consonants which blend together in words. Examples of blends are: *cl* as clap, claw, clip, class; *gl* as in glass, glare, gleem; *fr* as in free, from, frank; *st* as in street, stripe, stroke; *bl* as in blue, black, blow.

Directions: Digraph and Blend Sounds

1.   In Appendix C you will find the digraph and blend sounds. Hand Appendix C to your youngster. Point to the digraphs and say: "Give me the sound these two letters make together."

sh   th   wh   ch

2.   As your child reads the sound of each digraph, record the wrong responses on a separate sheet of paper. This will tell you which digraphs your child needs to work on.

3.   Now point to the blends, saying, "Give me the sound these two letters make together."

dr	fl	wr	fr	tr	br	cl
sl	gl	sw	gr	dw	sm	bl
pl	pr	st	tw	sp		

4.   Repeat the procedure for recording wrong responses.

Summary of Phonics Skills

1. Did your child know all of the consonant sounds?

    _____

2. Did your child know all of the vowel sounds?

    _____

3. Did your child know all of the digraphs?

    _____ If not, which digraphs were

    troublesome? _____

4. Did your child know all of the blends?

    _____ If not, which blends were

    troublesome? _____

MEASURING WORD RECOGNITION SKILLS

You will need to know at what level your child can look at words and pronounce them quickly and accurately. In this case, you do *not* want to determine your child's ability to "sound them out."

To test word recognition skills, you may say to your child, "read all of the words in the first column," which are in Appendix D, *Words*. After the words in the first column have been read, proceed as far as your child can possibly go, even if many mistakes are being made. Continue until five words have been missed in succession. Remember, at this point you are only checking word recognition level.

Directions

1. Having determined your child's independent reading level from the oral reading measurement, you can start him or her on the word recognition list at that level. For example, if you have found your child's independent reading to be at a first grade level, hand Appendix D to him or her and say, "Let me hear you read all of the words in the No. 2 column."

2. If all words are read correctly, have your child continue reading at successively higher levels until five words are missed in a row.

3. If your child misses more than five words in the column you have selected, ask him or her to read easier levels until you reach one in which all words are read quickly and accurately. The level just above this is the one at which your child should begin practicing word recognition exercises.

4. As your child reads each word, notice and record whether he or she stumbles over beginning sounds, ending sounds, or middle sounds. Listen as more difficult words are read, to find out whether the child is attempting to break words apart and sound them out, or making wild guesses based on the general configuration of the word. Record words missed and note types of errors.

Summary of Word Recognition

1. At what level was your youngster able to read all of the words quickly and accurately?

    _____

2. Did your child stop to look at each letter as an attempt was made to sound them out?

    _____

3. Were beginning sounds known, but not ending sounds? _____

4. Were ending sounds known, but not beginning sounds? _____

5. Did your youngster break words apart and sound them out? _____

6. Did your youngster take wild guesses at words and not look at them carefully? _____

    If so, which ones? _____

PART C

DEVELOPING YOUR CHILD'S READING SKILLS

6

Selecting Reading Materials

By now, you should have a good idea of your child's reading problems. However, before you begin tutoring with your youngster, it will be necessary to know the most appropriate reading materials available. In this chapter you will review:

- **The Importance of Selecting the Right Books**

- **How to Use Your Library**

- **What to Tell and Not Tell Your Child About Books**

- **A Listing of Suggested Books, Graded from Pre-First Through Seventh Grade Levels**

It is imperative that you be well organized in what you are going to do each time you have a tutoring session with your child. Being prepared with books that your child will find interesting is a part of being well organized.

THE IMPORTANCE OF YOUR SELECTION

The right reading materials are of crucial importance. If a fifth grader is reading at a first grade level, possibly the books he or she is being given are too "babyish" or boring. This can cause complete loss of interest in reading. Normally intelligent children can be humiliated by being asked to read low-level materials; they may simply laugh and refuse to try, even when they realize a teacher is sincerely trying to help them.

There are many high-interest but low-vocabulary books on the market today for helping older students who are reading at the first, second, third, or fourth grade level. A list featuring high-interest, low-vocabulary books appears at the end of this chapter.

YOUR PUBLIC LIBRARY

Your public library will help you and your child more than you can imagine. There are hundreds of books graded for limited vocabulary reading that hold strong appeal to the interests of older children. Take a trip to your library and explore the children's section. Many books on the list mentioned above are available to your child, since they are very popular with young readers.

You may wish to visit the library alone the first time, since your youngster may have already been "turned off" by unpleasant library experiences, or have been so defeated by reading that any attempts to arouse an interest in books would trigger only resistance. If you are unfamiliar with your library, ask the librarian for help. Most library workers are very interested in helping parents develop good reading habits in their children, and they are trained to do so.

Whatever you do, do not tell your child the books you have selected are going to be easy or "you will like this story"; let these facts become a pleasant surprise to you both, after the actual reading practice begins. Once your child discovers that reading can be actually enjoyable, he or she will want to select reading materials independently. This is the first big goal you can accomplish.

At the library, choose from the suggested list at the end of this chapter a couple of books that you are sure your child will enjoy hearing read aloud. Remember, it is absolutely essential that you start at a very easy reading level. At this point, you are merely preparing yourself and getting organized for your child's own specially designed reading program.

The books you have selected will be used for two purposes: recreational reading and instruction. It will be necessary for the child to know most of the words to begin with, so that he or she can read aloud to you with some degree of success. If the book you have selected turns out to be too difficult, you should put it aside until your young reader is ready to master the words with a minimum of prompting.

Most any book will have words that need to be taught first. If you have selected the book, *Cowboy Sam*, then you will need to say the title of the book. Chances are when your youngster then sees the words *Cowboy Sam* in the book, they will be remembered.

Begin by centering your instruction around the book you have chosen for both interest and reading level. Using the above-mentioned book as an example, if your child does not know his or her sounds, you may start with the letter "s" as in Sam. Have the student relate the "s" sound to as many words as the two of you can think of, and give generous praise for accomplishment.

Easy reading materials are constructed to use repetition of words in a meaningful manner. There are many children who need to see words over and over before they can remember them; such books use repetition while keeping interest level high. Much necessary letter-drill may be quite dull for your child, therefore the reading of the book should be made fun and exciting. It is up to you to help make the book exciting. You can speculate about what is going to happen next, examine pictures in chapters ahead, or use methods of your own to help maintain interest in the story.

SUGGESTED BOOKS

PRE-FIRST

Title of Book and Author

JERRY, Battle
DAN FRONTIER, Hurley
DAN FRONTIER AND THE NEW HOUSE,
    Hurley
BUCKY BUTTON, McCall
SAILOR JACK, Wasserman
SAILOR JACK AND EDDY, Wasserman
SAILOR JACK AND HOMER POTTS,
    Wasserman

FIRST GRADE

Title of Book and Author

JERRY GOES FISHING, Battle
JERRY GOES RIDING, Battle
COWBOY SAM, Chandler
COWBOY SAM AND PORKY, Chandler
COWBOY SAM AND SHORTY, Chandler
DOG PALS, Dolch
TOMMY'S PETS, Dolch
ZOO IN HOME, Dolch
NOBODY LISTENS TO ANDREW, Guilfoile
DAN FRONTIER GOES HUNTING, Hurley
DAN FRONTIER WITH THE INDIANS, Hurley
THE BUTTONS AT THE FARM, McCall
THE BUTTONS AND THE PET PARADE.
   McCall
JIM FOREST AND RANGER DAN, Rambeau
JIM FOREST AND THE BANDITS, Rambeau
SAILOR JACK AND BLUEBELL, Wasserman
SAILOR JACK'S NEW FRIEND, Wasserman

SECOND GRADE

Title of Book and Author

JUST BE PATIENT, Angelo
JERRY GOES ON A PICNIC, Battle
COWBOY SAM AND FREDDY, Chandler
COWBOY SAM AND THE RODEO, Chandler
THE SEA HUNT, Coleman
TREASURE UNDER THE SEA, Coleman
PETER AND THE UNLUCKY ROCKET,
    Corson
ANIMAL STORIES, Dolch
DOG STORIES, Dolch
CIRCUS STORIES, Dolch
FOLK STORIES, Dolch
HORSE STORIES, Dolch
IRISH STORIES, Dolch
PUEBLO STORIES, Dolch
WHY STORIES, Dolch
DANNY AND THE DINOSAUR, Hoff
A BIG BALL OF STRING, Holland
DAN FRONTIER AND THE WAGON TRAIN,
    Hurley
A FLY WENT BY, McClintock
COME ALONG, McKee
ON WE GO, McKee

A MAN NAMED COLUMBUS, Norman
JOHNNY APPLESEED, Norman
JIM FOREST AND THE MYSTERY HUNTER,
  Rambeau
JIM FOREST AND DEAD MAN'S PEAK,
  Rambeau
THE CAT IN THE HAT, Seuss
THE CAT IN THE HAT COMES BACK, Seuss
SAILOR JACK AND THE TARGET SHIP,
  Wasserman

THIRD GRADE

Title of Book and Author

GREAT MOMENTS IN AMERICAN HISTORY,
  Allen
PILOT JACK KNIGHT, Anderson and Johnson
JERRY GOES TO THE CIRCUS, Battle
CHIEF BLACK HAWK, Beale
LEAF THE LUCKY, Berry
THE FIVE CHINESE BROTHERS, Bishop
COWBOY SAM AND THE INDIANS, Chandler
COWBOY SAM AND THE RUSTLERS,
  Chandler
SUBMARINE RESCUE, Coleman

ABRAHAM LINCOLN, Colver
TOMMY O'TOOLE AND THE FOREST FIRE,
    Cordts
PETER AND THE MOON TRIP, Corson
PETER AND THE TWO-HOUR MOON, Corson
PETER AND THE ROCKET SHIP, Corson
AESOP'S STORIES, Dolch
ANDERSEN STORIES, Dolch
FAIRY STORIES, Dolch
FAR EAST STORIES, Dolch
GREEK STORIES, Dolch
IVANHOE, Dolch
ROBIN HOOD STORIES, Dolch
STORIES FROM JAPAN, Dolch
STORIES FROM MEXICO, Dolch
GEORGE WASHINGTON CARVER, Epstein
BETSY'S LITTLE STAR, Haywood
AFTER THE SUN SETS, Huber
DAN FRONTIER - SHERIFF, Hurley
RIDDLES, RIDDLES, RIDDLES,
    Leeming and Miller
A TREASURE CHEST OF HUMOR, Mellon
JIM FOREST AND LONE WOLF GULCH,
    Rambeau
JIM FOREST AND THE FLOOD, Rambeau
THE MYSTERY OF MORGAN CASTLE,
    Rambeau

CURIOUS GEORGE, Rey
DOORWAYS TO ADVENTURE,
    Shane and Hester
SAILOR JACK GOES NORTH, Wasserman
DANIEL BOONE, Wilkie

FOURTH GRADE

Title of Book and Author

BLAZE FINDS THE TRAIL, Anderson
MR. POPPER'S PENGUINS, Atwater
THE HIDDEN GARDEN, Bennett
A DOG FOR DAVIE'S HILL, Bice
STAR BOY, Biemiller
RODEO ROUNDUP, Bjorklund
FIRST MEN IN SPACE, Clark
HENRY HIGGINS, Cleary
TREASURE AT FIRST BASE, Clymer
PINOCCHIO, Collodi
STATE TROOPER, Gates
CROSS-COUNTRY TRUCKER, Gates
KEEPERS OF THE LIGHTS, Gates
DENNIS THE MENACE, Ketcham
BABY SITTER'S GUIDE BY DENNIS THE
    MENACE, Ketcham

KING ARTHUR AND HIS KNIGHTS,
    Kottmeyer
ROBIN HOOD STORIES, Kottmeyer
MISS PICKERELL AND THE GEIGER
    COUNTER, MacGregor
THE SNAKE THAT WENT TO SCHOOL,
    Moore
THE MYSTERY OF THE MISSING MARLIN,
    Rambeau
ROADS TO EVERYWHERE, Russell
STORIES FOR TODAY'S YOUTH, Schleyer
IF I RAN THE ZOO, Seuss
YERTLE THE TURTLE, Seuss
ARROW BOOK OF JOKES AND RIDDLES,
    Withers
FRANKLIN ROOSEVELT, Weil
THE UNINVITED DONKEY, White

FIFTH AND SIXTH GRADES

Title of Book and Author

STAGE COACH DRIVER, Chandler
CIRCUS TRAIN, Chandler
COWBOY ON THE TRAIL, Russell
COWBOY SOLDIER, Russell

SAILOR JACK GOES NORTH,
    Wasserman, Fraser
MOONBEAM AND SUNNY, Wasserman
ALLEY ALLIGATOR AND THE HUNTER,
    Packer, Cliett
PETER AND THE ROCKET SHIP, Corson
PETER AND THE TWO HOUR MOON, Corson
PETER AND THE MOON TRIP, Corson

SIXTH AND SEVENTH GRADES

Title of Book and Author

WITH WORLD HEROES, Dawson
COWBOY MARSHALL, Russell
DAN FRONTIER GOES TO CONGRESS,
    Hurley
MYSTERY ADVENTURE
    OF THE TALKING STATUES, Bamman,
        Kennedy, Whitehead
    OF THE JEWELED BELL, Bamman,
        Kennedy, Whitehead
    AT THE CAVE FOUR, Bamman,
        Kennedy, Whitehead
    OF THE INDIAN BURIAL, Bamman,
        Kennedy, Whitehead

MYSTERY ADVENTURE
   AT LONG CLIFF INN,
      Bamman, Kennedy, Whitehead
   OF THE SMUGGLED TREASURE
      Bamman, Kennedy, Whitehead
World of Adventure Series
   LOST URANIUM MINE,
      Bamman, Whitehead
   FLIGHT TO THE SOUTH POLE,
      Bamman, Whitehead
   HUNTING GRIZZLY BEARS,
      Bamman, Whitehead
   FIRE ON THE MOUNTAIN,
      Bamman, Whitehead
   CITY BENEATH THE SEA,
      Bamman, Whitehead
   THE SEARCH FOR PIRANHA,
      Bamman, Whitehead
   THE SACRED WELL OF SACRIFICE,
      Bamman, Whitehead
   VIKING TREASURE,
      Bamman, Whitehead
Racing Wheels Series:
   HOT ROD, Dean
   DESTRUCTION DERBY, Dean
   DRAG RACE, Dean
   STOCK CAR RACE, Dean

Racing Wheels Series:
 ROAD RACE, Dean
 INDY 500, Dean
Sports Mystery Series:
 TEN FEET TALL, Lunemann
 NO TURNING BACK, Lunemann
 FAIRWAY DANGER, Lunemann
 TIP OFF, Lunemann
 PITCHER'S CHOICE, Lunemann
 FACE OFF, Lunemann
 SWIMMER'S MARK, Lunemann
 TENNIS CHAMP, Lunemann
Space Science Fiction Series:
 SPACE PIRATE, Bamman, O'Dell,
  Whitehead
 MILKY WAY, Bamman, O'Dell,
  Whitehead
 BONE PEOPLE, Bamman, O'Dell,
  Whitehead
 PLANET OF THE WHISTLERS, Bamman,
  O'Dell, Whitehead
 INVISO MAN, Bamman, O'Dell,
  Whitehead
 ICE-MEN OF RIME, Bamman, O'Dell,
  Whitehead
NOW HEAR THIS, Dawson, Newman, Benthul
PLANS AND THE FUTURE, Gehrman, Stanek

DRUGS AND YOUR LIFE, Afterman, Sanders
IT'S YOUR LIFE, Pancrazio
Play the Game Geries:
    CLIMB ANY MOUNTAIN, McAdam
    THE SKILLFUL WHIP, McAdam
    HOLDUP AT THE CROSSOVER,
        McAdam
    MORE THAN SPEEDY WHEELS,
        McAdam
    FORTY FOR SIXTY, McAdam
    VIVA GONZALES, McAdam
    CHIEF CLOUD OF DUST, McAdam
    BULL ON ICE, McAdam
FIRE GUARD, Dixon
FAST SNOW, Dixon

Some of the simplified classics which may interest your child are:

ROBINSON CRUSOE (Random House), Defoe
ROBINSON CRUSOE (Garrard), Defoe
ROBIN HOOD (Webster), Kottmeyer
SIX GREAT STORIES (Scott, Foresman)
    Moderow

7

Developing
Comprehension Skills

In one sense, this may be the most important chapter in this book. Developing comprehension skills means to develop the ability to understand or grasp what words, phrases and sentences mean in their context. Obviously, to comprehend what is meant by sets of letters arranged in various ways is the main purpose of reading.

In this chapter you will review five areas that are crucial for comprehension, along with our suggestions for developing particular skills. These areas concern:

- **Using Oral Reading Exercises**

- **Using Silent Reading Exercises**

- **The Use of Questions for Review**

- **Developing Reading Objectives**

- **Teaching to Follow Directions**

ORAL READING

The oral method is not the most desirable one for teaching reading, but it does serve to keep you in touch with how much learning is being retained by the child. Many children learn to read without paying attention to what they are reading; thus their comprehension is poor. Such children are referred to as "word callers." They can read words very well, even at a high level, but they have not learned to think about what they have read.

Be a Good Listener

In addition, as their skills improve, children love to have someone listen to them read; and it takes a while for them to get in the habit of reading to themselves. Therefore, it is advisable to incorporate both oral and silent reading in the practice sessions you have with your child.

How Much Help to Give

It must be emphasized that if you find it necessary to pronounce more than three or four words on a page during oral reading, the book you are using is too advanced for the reader's present skills, and it will be wise to abandon it for easier materials.

If you go through the story yourself before presenting it to your child, you should be able to anticipate difficulty with certain words. These words might be taught to the child before he or she starts reading the story. Following is a simple example of this technique.

Suppose you intend to introduce a story that begins:

> John had a brown dog.
> His name was Flip.
> He ran away one day.
> John found him in a yard far away.

You may have previously determined that your child has difficulty with "sight" words—those which should already be known from memory. In this case you would review words such as *had, his, was* and *away* with the child before starting the story. On the other hand, if you have found the youngster is well grounded on such basic words, but has trouble with sounding out new ones, you would use phonic clues to teach the words *brown, name, ran, found* and *yard*. (If it turns out the child is already familiar with words you have chosen for drill, checking them out will still serve a double purpose; it will assure you that the child's reading will be quick and accurate, and bolster his or her self-reliance in tackling the materials.)

You will be surprised at the confidence a child develops after becoming able to read an entire page without help. Prior word practice will also help the child avoid being forced to labor over individual words.

SILENT READING

Children in the first and second grades find it difficult to sit down at home and read a book by themselves. They love to have other family members sit with them as they read story after story. Even if you do get them to sit by themselves and read, they often read aloud (usually within earshot of someone else). Don't discourage your child from reading like this; it is a necessary part of learning to read and it adds to the satisfaction of having accomplished such a remarkable task.

To begin silent reading practice, select a story you would like your child to read. Interest can be developed by telling him or her something about it—just enough to arouse a little excitement.

After the reading is completed, say, "Now tell me everything you have read." It is wise to try to get the child in the habit of recalling details without a great deal of prompting. Once your child has told you what he or she has remembered, you might ask one or two questions. It is important to stress meanings; after all, that is the purpose of learning to read.

There are children who have a tendency to get the order of events in a story confused, who will retell what they have just read by starting at the ending or midpoint, or by confusing the order of events in some other way. If your child does this, review the story by asking, "What happened first?" And help him or her to recall the correct train of events with questions indicating your interest in the story rather than an obvious attempt to force "right answers."

However, if this method of review fails to help the child remember a story in logical order, you might present a series of questions that follow the story line exactly, which will serve as a model for development of orderly memory.

THE USE OF QUESTIONS FOR REVIEW

The series-of-questions approach described above is valuable in any comprehension exercise.

Going back to the paragraph presented earlier, after the child reads:

> John had a brown dog.
> His name was Flip.
> He ran away one day.
> John found him in a yard far away.

you might immediately ask, "What did John have?" "What was his name?" "What did the dog do?" "Did John find him?"

These very simple questions will, in all probability, be easily answered by the child. You can then proceed to a few "thought" questions, such as "Why do you suppose John named his dog Flip?" "Why do you think the dog ran away?" "What do you think John did when he found his dog?" "Do you think he was happy?"

Questions such as this, posed with a genuine show of interest in the child's response, serve to help the reader become involved in the story and are invaluable aids to comprehension—which is dependent on interest above all else.

In case you are working with a third grader and using first grade level materials, you will not have to be overly concerned with comprehension; nevertheless, the content of whatever has been read must be discussed to help the child for meaning from the very beginning.

DEVELOPING READING OBJECTIVES

Following is a list of suggestions to aid you in assisting your child to understand everything he or she reads:

1. Ask open-ended questions during the reading, such as, "What do you think will happen next?" (Follow up later with "Were you right?")

2. Have the child read to find out *why*.

3. Read until the child can tell you about one certain incident you have told him or her to anticipate in the story.

4. Ask for a prediction of what might happen at the end of a story.

5. Assure the child that reading is "talk written down" and that the words are merely words we

all use every day; therefore, reading always "tells"
the reader something.

6.　　Stress that reading is a thinking process.

The beginning of a lesson might go as follows. Say to
the child, "Look at the pictures on the page. What do you
think is happening?" "How do the characters feel?" "Can
you tell by their faces what they are thinking or how they
feel?"

You can also develop attention to detail by asking
questions, such as "What time of day do you think the picture shows?" "What season of the year?"

You do not always need to test comprehension. The
idea is to arouse interest, which will automatically develop
comprehension skills.

The main thing is to form habits of thinking while
reading. *Reading is thinking.*

At times, your child may pick up new words from
what teachers call "context clues," or recognizing a word
from the meaning of the rest of the sentence. Here is a
sample exercise that can be used to develop word identification through the use of context clues:

Rabbits live in _____ .
                    houses   woods   trees   streets

It is hot in the _____ .
                    winter   summer

Bears like_____ .
              honey   bees

At other times, a word can be identified from the contents of a picture illustrating the story; for example, if the book is about John and his airplane, and the illustration shows John in an airplane, the child will tend to pick up context clues for the word "airplane" from the picture.

Pictures and photographs can also be used to develop comprehension of abstract concepts, such as love, anger, friendship, sadness and happiness. Plentiful illustrations of abstract meanings can be found in magazines, newspapers and books. Discussion of these concepts can help you learn a great deal about your child's self-concept as well as his or her feelings concerning school, friends, home and the rest of the world; and this can aid you in understanding the way he or she behaves.

TEACHING HOW TO FOLLOW DIRECTIONS

Many children appear unable to follow more than one verbal direction at a time. While this may not at first glance seem relevant to reading comprehension, it is basic to all understanding of (and memory for) words and their meanings.

A common complaint of teachers and parents is voiced in the familiar sentence, "If you had listened to what I said, you'd have known what to do next." The key words here are *patience* and *practice.*

Rather than becoming increasingly exasperated with a child who fails to follow a sequence of directions, you can turn it into a game that will challenge the youngster and lend pleasure to his or her learning. Beginning with a simple request, such as "Please close the door," add to the number of directions gradually, finally arriving at a sentence like "Please close the door, hand me the paper, then pet the dog and give him his ball."

If not forced into this game too often, the child will enjoy mastering a series of directions while learning an extremely important comprehension skill.

8

Developing Listening Skills

In case you find your child has difficulty discriminating between sounds, it will be wise to spend time developing this skill at the beginning of your instruction. Sometimes a child's inability to sound out words is caused by a lack of knowing how to distinguish between sounds as they are spoken. Sometimes poor listening habits are responsible. However, there are a number of techniques and strategies for developing auditory discrimination skills and good listening habits.

In this chapter you will review:

- **Techniques for Improving Auditory Discrimination**

- **The Importance of Listening Habits**

- **Games for Listening Skill Development**

AUDITORY DISCRIMINATION

Teaching auditory discrimination will be along the same lines as the test that measures this skill. First of all, say two words and ask your child to tell you if you said the same word or different words. Here are some words you can use; you will undoubtedly wish to add others after you have identified the student's individual trouble spots in this area. You will note that this list includes some pairs of words that are in fact identical.

ball - bat	what - where
bean - been	why - why
big - dog	shall - shell
cat - come	be - big
was - saw	crab - crib
this - them	gang - gang
that - that	here - where

Should you discover that your child does not pay attention to ending sounds, give groups of words with similar and different ending consonants. Examples:

cat - cook	dog - dot	flat - flop
hot - hook	drip - drill	got - gone
bat - ball	ear - eat	run - rut
blue - blue	fat - far	sat - sap

The same kind of exercise can be used to test discrimination of beginning consonants. Examples:

ran - man	fall - fell	have - very
pet - take	brush - crush	jack - pack
sell - chill	day - dog	let - met
neat - meat	girl - curl	tip - ten

Difficulty in distinguishing middle sounds (usually vowels) also can be determined by this method. Examples:

some - same	shave - shove	shave - have
mat - met	rang - ring	joke - folks
love - dove	bill - hill	ball - bell
right - rate	live - laugh	ten - tin

As you work on auditory skills, you may discover that your child is able to hear the sounds accurately, but merely has been inattentive to previous instruction.

LISTENING HABITS

The first and foremost way to teach listening habits is to be a good listener yourself. When your children talk to you, look into their eyes and give them your individual attention. *Do not interrupt*; listen to all they have to say, then ask questions and listen to the answers. One of parents' frequent mistakes is in talking *at* their children instead of *with* them.

Most classroom teachers have developed many techniques for teaching children to listen. Teachers recognize that in order to teach children, they must be able to hold their attention. One way to accomplish this is through games that require listening.

GAMES FOR SKILL DEVELOPMENT

Game I

Remember the game "Simon Says" we played as children? It is a particularly good one for teaching listening skills.

The person who is "it" issues directions, as rapidly as possible, for the others to follow, using the words "Simon Says" as a gimmick to trap his listeners into making a mistake. For example, when the teacher declares, "Simon says thumbs up!" everyone is supposed to put thumbs up; but if the command is simply "Thumbs up!" or "Thumbs down!," anyone who follows it must drop out of the game (or—if only two are playing—must take the part of "it"). Additional short commands (not longer than two or three words) such as "Stand up!," "Sit down!," "Close your eyes!," and "Laugh!" or "Cry!" may be used to make the game more complicated for older children. The main thrust of the exercise is rapid delivery of commands, which forces careful attention to listening.

Game II

Both you and your child close your eyes, then try to identify everything you can hear. Let your child start naming sounds, then add to the list with additional ones he or she has missed. (Someone is hammering, cars are passing by, a pencil is being tapped, a horn is blowing, or a bird is chirping.) Let your child compete with you in listening for more detailed discrimination, such as whether a vehicle going by is a car or a truck, what kind of bird might be chirping, or even who might be doing the hammering.

Game III

Another old favorite game starts with the person playing "it" stating, "I am going to the moon and I am going to take along something that begins with _____"—filling the blank with a letter from the alphabet. As the game proceeds from one player to the next, each player names all the words already called that begin with the same letter, then adds a new one. This game (an excellent one for car traveling) can be varied by starting with a word from the leader that begins with "a" and requiring successive players to call out words beginning with the other letters of the alphabet, in exact order, after repeating each word that has already been called. (Example: apple, ball, cat, dog, elephant—and on through the alphabet.) Any players failing to recall all words in proper sequence would drop out until the winner (or the one who remembers most) is left, to become "it" for the next round.

Game IV

Here is a game called "rhythms" that not only teaches a child to listen, but in addition helps him or her to categorize objects and to follow directions. The person who is "it" calls out a category such as states, automobiles, flowers, fruits, cities, animals, etc., and sets up a rhythm by clapping hands or snapping fingers—which all players are expected to follow, by keeping time as they take turns naming things in the category that have been established. The rhythm is kept going and anyone unable to call out the name of something in the same category must drop out. The player staying in the game until all others have dropped out becomes "it" for the next game.

Game V

Another game requires players to remember a missing word in a sentence. Say a complete sentence, such as "Father went to the store to buy a hammer, nails, and a saw." Now repeat the sentence and leave out a word. The object is to have your child recall the word you omitted. "Father went to the _____ to buy a hammer, nails, and a saw." Build sentences yourself and see how complicated you can make them. Children love this game, which can be varied by reversing rules with the child—letting him or her make up the sentence with missing words for you to guess.

Game VI

Practice with consonant sounds is furnished by the game, "I am thinking of a word that begins like _____ (naming any word that begins with a consonant). Each player is expected to name a word beginning with the same consonant sound (not necessarily the same letter). Players drop out when they miss and the final survivor becomes "it."

Game VII

A game using words that rhyme is a variation of the above. Use sentences like, "It is yellow and *sounds* like stencil. What is it?" The player who gives the first answer gets to ask for the next rhyming word.

9

Developing Phonetic Skills

Before you begin, buy yourself a felt tip pen and a pad of paper, or a chalk and chalkboard. Keep them handy so that both you and your child can use them as you work together. Now that you are sure that your child can hear all of the sounds, you will want to begin to associate the sound with the printed symbol, to teach what the sounds "look like."

Let us stress here that the procedure for teaching phonic skills normally stretches over the first three grades, so don't think you have to teach them all in a month. It is much better for a child to master skills one at a time than to be bombarded by everything at once.

In this chapter you will review:

- **Games for Teaching Beginning Consonants**

- **How to Teach the Confusing "b" and "d"**

- Exercises and Games for Teaching Long and Short Vowels

- Exercises and Games for Teaching Digraphs and Blends

TEACHING BEGINNING CONSONANT SOUNDS

There are many very simple alphabet cards and books on the market today that teach beginning sounds.

Consonant Games

1.   Sesame Street has created many books and other materials which are inexpensive and entertaining for children of many ages. The characters are comic in form. One in particular, *The Sesame Street Book of Letters*, teaches each sound with a jingle and also shows where the letter fits into the alphabet. For example, in teaching the letter "h," the jingle goes, "Is Happy Harry Hidden in His Hole?" Beside it is a picture of Harry in a manhole.

Using this type of material to teach beginning sounds is certainly a lot more fun for the child than to isolate sounds which have no connection with actual words.

2.   Teaching letter sounds by attaching them to words will make letter sounds meaningful to your youngster. You should use words, as much as possible, from your child's own vocabulary.

For example, if you are teaching the letter sound "b," show the "b." Then with a pen or pencil, write down all of the "b" words your child can think of. If there is difficulty at first, you may need to think of some words and write them down to get the game started. (Don't expect your child to know how to spell each word; that will have to come later.) Write down such words as ball, bag, bat, be, beautiful, brown, basket, etc.

This procedure should be used with each letter your child needs to learn. Remember, at this point you are teaching only the beginning sounds; don't try to confuse your youngster with ending or middle sounds at this time. Try to help him or her master one beginning sound at a time. Don't go too fast and don't become frustrated if some forgetting takes place. Constant reviewing is a necessity here because you have a long way to go, and it is very easy for a child to confuse sounds.

3.   There are word games available in book stores or in supermarkets, consisting of sets of cards with letters and pictures. The object of such a game is for the child to

match the correct letter with the picture. If you are creative, you can also make your own, following this example:

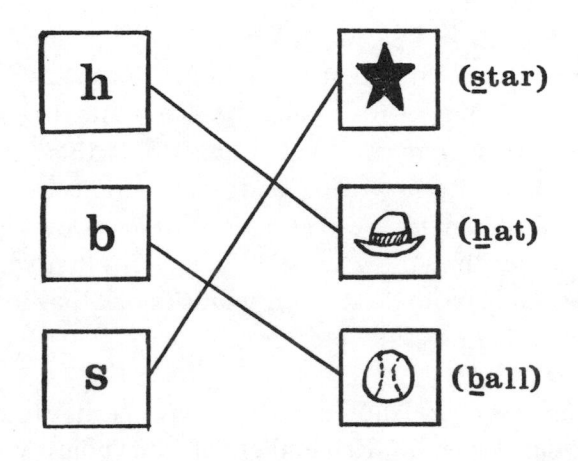

4.   Here are some exercises you may also use. On a
large sheet of paper write:

dog	big	bat	run
cry	came	sat	bite
boat	boy	can	coat

Now say, "*cat* and *come*—I am going to say three
words and you draw a circle around the one that begins
like *cat* and *come*."

Have your child draw a circle around the words that begin like the word you pronounce. After you have completed the lesson, go over the material with the youngster. He or she need not know all of the words, but say them anyway; thus beginning sounds become meaningful.

On another sheet of paper write the following:

boy	see	and	up
cat	bat	run	sit
here	sat	big	bait

Now say, "I am going to say three words and you draw a circle around the word that begins like *box* and *book*." If the child becomes confused, repeat the directions; praise each success; and give help as many times as necessary, until the child has mastered all consonant sounds.

THE CONFUSING "b" and "d"

The two consonants most confusing to beginners are *b* and *d* because these letters exactly reverse one another.

To impress both the shapes and sounds of these letters, print the word *bed.* Draw a light line over the *e*
(between *b* and *d*) to produce a rough picture of a bed,
with the headboard and footboard represented by the two
letters.

bed

This presents an association to which the child can
always refer, whenever he is having trouble remembering
the name of either letter, or its sound.

TEACHING VOWEL SOUNDS

Teaching vowel sounds and their rules is often the
most difficult and tedious task for a parent, but if you pre-
pare a lesson ahead of time and know just what material
and procedures you will use, it may be less painful. As
stated before, you should work only a short time during
the reading session. There are many helpful materials on
the market today. You may find out what is available by
checking your bookstore or asking the child's teacher.

The Letter "a"

Begin with the letter "a" and master it thoroughly.

1.   The letter "a" has a short and long sound. The word *apple* is said to have a short "a" sound. The letter "a" in the word *gate* is said to have a long "a" sound. Probably the best way to impress the long "a" sound (as well as other long vowels) is by teaching that "long 'a' says its name."

2.   Work with the child on a list of words containing the long "a" sound—such as gate, mate, sale, cake, nail, pail.

3.   Turning to the short "a" sound, make another list of short words containing it—such as bag, bat, ball, bad, back, can, cat, car.

A word of caution: before each new session, review skills taught in the previous lesson. If you find the child has not mastered those skills, don't show discouragement or disappointment. If you express any negative attitudes at the beginning of a new session, the child will tend to become discouraged and less cooperative.

After you have listed many words containing short "a" and long "a" sounds, you can move to helping the child discover the general rules covering these two sounds, using the following procedures.

General Rules and Procedures

1. Have your child say all of the words which he or she can think of that make the sound of a short "a"—such as bag, ball, bad, back, can, cat, car. Make a long list of the words together.

2. Think of all the long "a" sounds—gate, mate, sale, cake, nail, pail.

Say the word *mat.* Is the "a" long or short?

    mat - (short "a" sound)

Say the word *cap.* Is the "a" long or short?

    cap - (short "a" sound)

Now write the word *cap* and add an "e" at the end - *cape.* Is the "a" in *cape* long or short? (long)

Say the word *car.* Is the "a" long or short?

car - (short "a" sound)

Now write the word *car* and add an "e" at the end - *care.* Is the "a" in *care* long or short? (long)

You might use the same procedure for mad-made, at-ate, fat-fate, fad-fade, gap-gape, past-paste.

After you have gone over many of these exercises, you will need to present the rule for the "a" changing from a short to long sound. (The word also changes completely.) You will notice that when you added the "e" at the end of each word, you did not hear the "e" sound. The "e" is said to be silent.

The two of you should be able to see the rule which applies to the long "a" sound. **RULE**: If a one-syllable word ends with a silent "e," then the preceding vowel sound is long. If there are two vowels in a one-syllable word, the first vowel is long and the second vowel is silent. Say the following words and listen for the long "a" sound: sail, pail, nail, jail, paint, bait, wait.

The Other Vowels

After he or she has mastered the long and short "a" sound, proceed to the long and short sound of "e." List as many words with long and short "e" as possible. The rules which applied to the long and short "a" will also apply to the long and short "e," "i," "o," and "u." Remember—if a one-syllable word has two vowels, the first one is long—such as flea, seat, sea, ear.

The following lists illustrate the rule for the other long and short vowels:

Long "e"	Short "e"
we	beg
see	peg
flea	leg
seat	let
seed	bet
free	met
tree	wet
cheek	set
ear	pet

Long "i"	Short "i"
vine	bid
like	lid
smile	pig
mine	big
dime	is
spite	it
lime	in
dried	rid

Long "o"	Short "o"
bone	cot
boat	dot
coat	got
door	hot
floor	not
load	pot
no	rot
poor	lot
roar	tot

Long "u"	Short "u"
mule	cup
lure	run
lute	sun
huge	sugar
cute	put
fuse	surf
fuel	mum
fruit	lug
suit	luck

Be sure to go over the above rules and procedures many times so that your child is able to apply them to words.

TEACHING CONSONANT
BLEND AND DIGRAPH SOUNDS

After your child has mastered the consonant and vowel sounds, it will be helpful to make sure he or she learns the consonant digraphs and initial blends. Digraphs are combinations of consonants that produce one sound. The digraphs are sh, th, wh, ch. The consonant blends are dr, fl, wr, fr, tr, br, cl, sl, gl, sw, gr, dw, sm, bl, pl, pr, st, tw, sp—in other words, two sounds that blend together.

Needless to say, this skill is also quite difficult for the child to master and remember. The mastery of these sounds may take a while, but have patience and stick with it.

Digraph and Blend Exercises

If you have purchased a set of word cards in which you match the sound with a picture, the publishers may have also included the digraphs and blends.

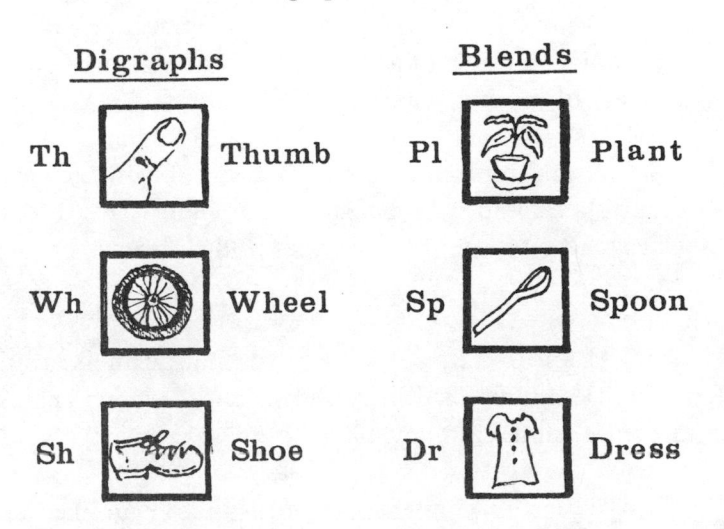

Digraphs			Blends		
Th		Thumb	Pl		Plant
Wh		Wheel	Sp		Spoon
Sh		Shoe	Dr		Dress

If they haven't, see how creative you can be; make your own. A child will appreciate this kind of effort on your part and may wish to help you think of examples.

Seeing you putting your energies into helping him or her learn will inspire the student to cooperate.

Digraph and Blend Games

After blends and digraphs have been taught, the child can practice distinguishing between the two. You might play games such as the following:

1.   I am thinking of some words that begin like *bl*ue. (Have the child think of a word that also begins like blue.) Examples: black, blow, bloom, block, blond, blink, blank.

2.   I am thinking of some words that begin like *br*ain (br sound). Examples: braid, brake, branch, brave, bread, break, breath, breeze, brew, bribe, bridge, broad, broom, brush.

3.   I am thinking of some words that begin like *ch*air (ch sound). Examples: chair, cheek, cheer, cherry, chess, chest, chief, chill, chimney, chip.

4.   I am thinking of some words that begin like *cl*am (cl sound). Examples: clamp, class, clean, clear, clip, cling, cliff, close, cloud, club.

5. I am thinking of some words that begin like *cr*ab (cr sound). Examples: cradle, crack, crash, crate, cream, creep, crew, crib, crow.

6. I am thinking of some words that begin like *dr*aw (dr sound). Examples: drink, drain, drive, drill, drop, drove, dry.

7. I am thinking of some words that begin like *fl*ag (fl sound). Examples: flame, flap, flare, flash, flat, flavor, flew, flight, float, floor, flower, fly, flush, flyer.

8. I am thinking of some words that begin like *fr*ame (fr sound). Examples: free, freedom, freeze, freight, fresh, friend, from, front, frost, frown, fry.

9. I am thinking of some words that begin like *gl*ass (gl sound). Examples: glider, globe, gloom, glossy, glory.

10. I am thinking of some words that begin like *gr*ade (gr sound). Examples: grain, grand, grape, grapefruit, grass, grave, gray, great, green, grime, grind, grocer, groom, ground, grow, grumble.

11. I am thinking of some words that begin like *pl*ace (pl sound). Examples: plain, plan, plane, planet, plank, plant, plastic, plate, play, please, pleasure, pledge, plum, plow, plump, plus.

12.   I am thinking of some words that begin like *pr*actice (pr sound). Examples: praise, pray, preach, price, print, private, prize, proof.

13.   I am thinking of some words that begin like *sc*ale (sc sound). Examples: scalp, scar, score, scare, scratch, scrape, scream, scribble.

14.   I am thinking of some words that begin like *sh*ade (sh sound). Examples: shake, sharp, shark, shave, shame, share, sheet, shelf, shell, shin, shine, ship, shift, shook, shop, short, should, shoulder, shrink, shut.

15.   I am thinking of some words that begin like *sk*ip (sk sound). Examples: ski, skid, skin, skim, skirt, sky, skunk.

16.   I am thinking of some words that begin like *sl*ack (sl sound). Examples: slam, slap, slash, slate, slain, slay, slid, sleep, slow, slide, slip, slot, slit, slug.

17.   I am thinking of some words that begin like *sm*all (sm sound). Examples: smack, smart, smell, smile, smooth, smoke.

18.   I am thinking of some words that begin like *sn*ag (sn sound). Examples: snake, snap, snatch, sneak, snip, snow, snug, snore, snort.

19.   I am thinking of some words that begin like *sp*ade (sp sound). Examples: spangle, spark, spare, spank, sparrow, spot, speak, spear, special, speck, speed, spell, spend, spider, spill, spin, spine, spirit, spit, splash, split, spoon, sponge, spool, sport, spray, sprinkle, sprout, spy.

20.   I am thinking of some words that begin like *st*ab (st sound). Examples: stable, stack, stage, stain, stair, stake, stamp, stand, star, start, state, stay, steak, steal, steam, still, stink, stir, stock, stole, stop, storm, strain, straight, stream, strike, strong, stripe, stunt.

21.   I am thinking of some words that begin like *sw*ab (sw sound). Examples: swallow, swamp, swap, swear, sweet, sweat, swift, swing.

22.   I am thinking of some words that begin like *th*ink (th sound). Examples: that, the, their, there, them, then, thermometer, thick, thieve, thin, thirty, thing, third, this, through, those, thousand, thread, threat, three, thrill, throat, thought, throw, thumb, thump, thunder.

23.   I am thinking of some words that begin like *tr*ace (tr sound). Examples: track, tractor, trade, traffic, trail, trailer, train, tramp, trap, trash, travel, tray, tread, treat, tree, trail, tribe, trick, trim, trip, trouble, troop, true, trunk, trust, try.

24.   I am thinking of some words that begin like *tw*elve (tw sound). Examples: twenty, twig, twin, twine, twinkle, twist.

25.   I am thinking of some words that begin like *wh*ale (wh sound). Examples: whack, what, wheat, wheel, when, where, whither, which, whip, while, whisper, white.

10

Developing
Word Recognition Skills

In this final chapter you will review a series of techniques, games, and rules for developing your child's ability to recognize words. You will review the following areas:

- Using the phonetics skills previously taught.

- Teaching "word families."

- Using larger units of sounds (syllables).

- Correcting reversals and other sight-reading problems.

- Teaching meanings of words.

- Using the dictionary.

- Using context clues.

- Developing a sight vocabulary.

- Some rules.

PHONETIC SKILLS:
THEIR ADVANTAGES AND PITFALLS

Children learn to identify words through knowledge of correct letter sounds, to use when new words are introduced. For example, when a child sees the word "hat" in a story, he or she will remember the "h," "a" and "t" sounds from other words. Identifying the word "hat" becomes easy because individual sounds have been mastered. But reading is not so easy when one must continually stop to go back through the process of letter-sounding.

One of the difficulties in teaching children to break words apart for "sounding out" is that they may become overanalytical. Such students will stop to analyze each word as they read, even though they have mastered them. Children who have had too much drill on letter sounds and word parts may fall into this habit; thus it is best to use a wide variety of approaches to reading.

It is advisable to work on word recognition separately from oral reading practice. Do not get your child into a continuous habit of sounding out words while reading. If he or she asks for help with a given word, pronounce the entire word immediately. If you say "sound it out," reading will become boring to your child and comprehension will be poor.

Also, there are children who become adept at breaking words apart, but cannot combine the separate sounds to pronounce the whole word. For example, if a child sees the word "hat," he or she might say "h" - "a" - "t," but be unable to blend the three sounds together into the word. If your child reads like this, *do not dwell on individual letter sounds*, as drill on words as whole units is the approach he or she needs.

Using flash cards will help a child look at the whole word quickly. You must remember, however, that flash cards can be made into a stimulating game—or they can be extremely tiresome—depending on how they are used.

On individual cards, write a set of words your child may already know. These may be words that the student has been "sounding out" on each encounter. For example, you might write:

this	come	home	put
that	dog	jump	run
what	eat	keep	sat
cat	fun	look	turn
apple	fast	man	van
ball	gone	not	where

Now say, "I am going to quickly show you a word. You tell me what the word is." If an incorrect word is called, say, "No, it is ____." Then proceed to the next word. Do not say "sound it out!"

LEARNING WORD FAMILIES

Children master word identification skills by learning word parts or "word families." The following exercises will help in teaching word parts.

Write the word "at." Now write consonants before "at" to make new words. (at - *h*at, *b*at, *c*at, *s*at, *r*at, *f*at, *m*at, *p*at, *v*at.)

Write the word "an." Write consonants before "an" to make new words. (an - *b*an, *c*an, *f*an, *m*an, *p*an, *t*an, *v*an.)

Write the word "and." Write consonants before "and" to make new words. (and - *b*and, *h*and, *l*and, *s*and.)

Write the word "it." Write consonants before "it" to make new words. (it - *b*it, *f*it, *h*it, *p*it, *s*it.)

LEARNING LARGER SOUND UNITS

To teach additional word parts, use an easy dictionary (preferably one written for children). Show your child how words are divided in the dictionary.

For example, look up the word "microscope." You will notice that it is divided as mi·cro·scope) and not m-i-c-r-o-s-c-o-p-e. You may then look up other words that have several syllables, such as mil·li·gram, min·i·mum, mis·tak·able, rec·i·pe, and rec·og·ni·tion and repeat the activity.

However, if this should prove too difficult at this time, don't dwell on it. Dictionaries should be fun for children. They open up a whole new world of words and ideas. It is up to you to make word study in dictionaries exciting and not punishment. Too often children are told to look up an unknown word in the dictionary, when they do not even know how to use one.

REVERSAL AND OTHER
SIGHT-READING PROBLEMS

A common reading problem encountered by specialists is the tendency of some children to reverse the order of letters in certain words. For example, a child may say "saw" for "was," "got" for "big," "tip" for "eat," "flip" for "cliff," and "that" for "what."

This type of reading difficulty may have been caused by too much emphasis on ending sounds. The student will look at the ending sound first, then perhaps the middle or the beginning. Some students may not have received instruction on the correct procedure for looking at words, so would habitually begin word identification by moving from right to left instead of left to right.

Correcting this type of problem isn't too difficult. Some exercises you might try are:

1. Have the child trace the word, pronounce it sound-by-sound, and spell it as he or she traces. This may be done with a pen, sandpaper words, or in sand. You should present the word first, then have your child go over it.

2. Do not dwell on word endings. For example, if you are going to teach the child to sound out the word "cat," introduce both the "a" and "t" sounds by relating them to beginnings of words.

3.   By the same token, don't overemphasize middle sounds or beginning sounds. This causes the child to focus on only one part of the word. For example, if the child does not pay attention to beginning sounds, errors such as saying "his" for "this," "all" for "fall," etc. could be made. If errors are made in the middle of words, the child may be looking at the beginning and ending sounds and neglecting the middle ones.

4.   Following is an exercise if your child looks at beginning sounds and then takes a guess at the rest of the word. By supplying the first letter of the desired word, you force your child to look at the middle and ending of each word presented.

a.   The man put on a h_____.

   hit   her   hat

b.   Children w_____ at school.

   play   work   read

c.   John likes to play b_____.

   catch   ball   marbles

d.   Br _____ me the book.

   Bring   Give   Hand

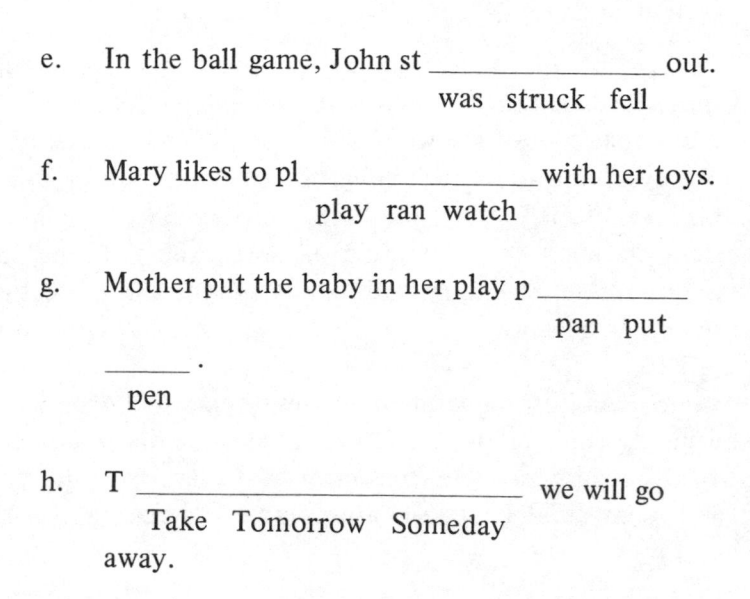

e.   In the ball game, John st _____out.

             was   struck   fell

f.   Mary likes to pl_____with her toys.

             play   ran   watch

g.   Mother put the baby in her play p _____

                             pan   put

_____ .

     pen

h.   T _____ we will go

         Take   Tomorrow   Someday

away.

WORDS HAVE MEANINGS

A student must learn that words have meanings. There are children who have developed such good phonetic skills that they think only about how a word looks and not what it "says." For example, children will read the word "was" as "wiz," "lip" as "leep," "finger" as "finer," etc.

A student might see a sentence such as "A dog had *spots* on his *back*," and read it, "A dog had *stops* on his *book*." Such a child has learned to read by taking a quick glance at the words without letting their meanings register in his or her mind. If there is a picture of a dog on the page, the student should be guided to look at it and tell about the dog. Ask, "Does the dog have a book or a back?" "What does the dog have on his back?"

We have on occasion seen students who will pick up a book and begin reading it rapidly without paying attention to any of the words. For example, a sentence such as, "A dog had spots on his back," might be read, "A girl went to the store."

As you work with your child, make sure you introduce new words by stressing their meaning as well as their sounds.

USING THE DICTIONARY

To help learn meanings of words, use your dictionary once again to discover together the enjoyment of learning all the meanings a word might have.

For example, look up some words that have several meanings.

You will find that *safe* is:

> a place to keep articles;
> freed from harm or risk; unhurt;
> successful in making a base in baseball;
> healthy; sound;
> cautious.

Love is:

> affection based on admiration;
> warm attachment;
> enthusiasm; devotion;
> a score of zero in tennis.

Band is:

> something that binds;
> a formal promise;
> a strip to hold things together;
> a cord across the backbone of a book;
> a ring of elastic;
> a strip of grooves on a phonograph record;
> to attach oneself to a group;
> to gather together.

USING CONTEXT CLUES

Children learn to identify words through the use of context clues. This means that if an entire sentence is read, the meaning of a particular word may be derived from the meaning of other words in the sentence.

Your child might see a sentence such as, "Bears like to eat *honey*." If the word *honey* is not immediately known, the rest of the sentence should have given a clue as to the meaning of the word.

Following is a group of sentences to use in teaching your child to use *context clues*. If there are two or more unknown words in a sentence, pronounce one of them yourself:

1.   We buy toys and books in *stores*.

2.   Boys and girls like to *read* books.

3.   Mother baked *cakes* and *cookies*.

4.   When there is a fire the *fire engine* comes.

5.   Dad likes to go *fishing* in the lake.

6.   John took his ball and mitt to the *baseball game*.

7.   We went in an *airplane* on our trip.

8.   A horse is a fast *animal.*

9.   In our garden we have *tomatoes, carrots,* and
      lettuce.

10.   John wants to be a *ghost* on *Halloween.*

DEVELOPING A BASIC SIGHT VOCABULARY

Emphasize to your child that certain words should be
memorized, or known by "sight." These words frequently
present problems to children and will need repetition before
they are a permanent part of their reading vocabulary. Children have trouble with these words because it is difficult
to attach meanings to them.

"Sight" words are part of every child's speaking vocabulary. Many of them are common prepositions and verb
forms. Following are examples of sight words your child
will encounter in reading:

about	must	is	not
around	like	it	your
and	the	to	when
at	of	which	this
before	off	should	that
between	in	want	these
but	at	be	those
come	will	not	got
what	able	some	have
where	for	him	said
why	once	her	here
whose	has	been	are
was	behind	again	soon
with	ask	had	give

Some reading teachers believe that children should memorize long lists of basic sight words. We do not feel this is necessary. If you find that particular words give your child trouble, write them on individual cards. Develop a card file of troublesome words. As you begin a new reading session, review the words on the cards.

The following exercise is an example of introducing basic sight words. Take a sentence such as, "Joe and Jane are here." The three basic sight words that should be known are *and, are,* and *here.* Before you have your child read the sentence, say, "There will be three words in the next sentence which will be hard to remember. These words are *and, are,* and *here.* Let's write each of them on separate cards, so we can remember them when we see them again."

Another useful activity is to write sentences, leaving a blank space for sight words. Encourage your child to say an appropriate word, then write it in the blank. (It is not necessary to have your child write the word at this point, unless you are sure he or she can spell it.)

Sentences you might use for this exercise are as follows. Select a word from the list of sight words presented on the preceding page, or write the words on cards and have your child choose the appropriate word among them. The words presented below the sentences are possible words to use.

1.   He ran _____

             around   behind   into   under   over the house.

2.   I will see you _____ .

             again   soon

3.   I will _____ you something.

         ask

4. John _____ Billy can play.
   and

5. Billy _____ home.
   came

6. I shall _____ you a ball.
   give

7. I shall _____ here.
   come

8. Billy _____ two balls.
   has   had

9. _____ is it?
   What   Where   When   Which   Who

10. Mary came _____ me.
    with

11. Billy _____ here.
    was

Make up other sentences if your child needs additional practice with sight words.

As you develop a card file of words, you will be able to use it many different ways.

1.   Write the same words on two different cards and use them to play "concentration."

2.   Reward each word remembered. Buy a small bank and as your child remembers words, put pennies (or nickles or dimes) in his or her bank. When enough money is saved, take a trip somewhere to buy something special.

3.   If words like *what, where, when, why, this, that, these* and *those* present particular difficulties, make up your own games to play, or use sentences such as the following. (Such words are probably the hardest words in the English language for children to remember.)

a.   *What* is *that?*

b.   I'll keep *these* and you take *those.*

c.   I'll take *this* one and you take *that* one.

d.   *Where* oh *where* has my little dog gone?

e.   *Why* did he go *there?*

f.   *When* will he come *here*?

One last word of caution: *do not have your child attempt to sound out* basic sight words.

If your student is going to be successful at reading, he or she must build up a large sight vocabulary—not just the small basic sight words, but as many words as possible. The importance of learning all of the word recognition techniques is to be able to look at a word quickly and identify it without relying on any one method for identification. When adults read they rarely think about letter sounds.

Even when a difficult word is encountered, a practiced reader will look at the entire word and not at its parts. Also, silent reading demands comprehension—not pronunciation. Children who stop to sound out each word tend to use lip movement while they are reading silently; this habit slows oral reading speed while it adds nothing to comprehension.

IMPORTANT RULES

Once your child has mastered the consonant and vowel sounds, and is beginning to master word recognition techniques, it will be wise to teach a few rules which should be of additional help in reading and spelling.

Endings Added to Words (ly, ed, ing, er, y)

1.   Write the word *sad*.

2.   If you want to write *sadder*, double the consonant "d" before adding *er*.

3.   The rule that applies here is:

When you have a one-syllable word with a final consonant and one vowel before it, the final consonant is doubled before adding an ending (er, est, ing, ed, y, est, etc.). *The final consonant must be heard.* For example, in the word "blowing," the "w" is not sounded; thus it is not doubled.

4.   Now for some practice.

a.   What endings have been added to the following words?

sit*ting*   bat*ter*
hit*ting*   trip*ping*
sad*der*   hot*ter*
fit*ting*   sip*ping*

b.   Write some words and let your child write the endings.

Doubling Consonants

The following words have two consonant sounds at the end; therefore, the final consonant is not doubled.

back_____   rest_____
sing_____   coach_____
pick_____   cold_____
pack_____   cast_____
fly_____   bang_____
flush_____   bind_____
nest_____   bank_____
test_____   assist_____

When the rule for doubling consonants is known, adding endings to other words will be easy.

Here are some more exercises for using the above rules.

1. Add "ing" to these words:

hit_____	sip_____
zip_____	fit_____
drop_____	stop_____
hop_____	dip_____

2. Add "est," "er," or "ed" to these words:

glad_____	big_____
sad_____	ship_____
mad_____	hit_____
fat_____	trip_____

Rule for Hard and Soft Sounds of "c"

The letter "c" confuses children because sometimes it has the sound of "k" and sometimes the sound of "s." Write and say the words cat, cook, cute, come, cent, city, ceiling, center, cell, cab, cash, cap, cot, cedar, and cement.

Help your child write the following rules: *If "c" comes before the vowels "a," "o," or "u," it has the hard*

sound of a "k." However, if "c" comes before "e" or "i,"
it has the soft sound of "s."

Rule for the Hard and Soft Sounds of "g"

The consonant "g" is another difficult letter for children. The letter "g" is hard in gate, go, got, game, guppy,
goose. It is soft in gem, German, geography, general, gentle,
and giant.

The rule for "g" is similar to the sound of "c," but
there are exceptions to watch, such as girl, give, get. *If "g"
comes before the vowels "a," "o," or "u," it is hard. It
is soft if it comes before "e" or "i."*

Remind your child that English pronunciations are
not always consistent, but that it does help to know what
the general rules are. Make a game of the inconsistencies,
rather than frustrating your child with them.

APPENDIX A

PARAGRAPHS FOR ORAL READING

PRIMER LEVEL

Peter went to see an old
wise man.
"What can I do?"
Peter asked the wise man.
"My house makes too
much noise.
My bed makes noise.
My door makes noise.
And my window makes noise".

LEVEL 1

Bobby had gone down the street
to say good-by to his friends.
He gave his goldfish
to his friend Jay.
He gave his turtle
to his friend Ben.
And he gave his frog
to his friend Mike.

LEVEL 2

Tammy had taken pictures of just about everything in the Rocky Mountains with her new camera. She wanted to show her friend Ann what it was like to go camping.

"Ann doesn't think camping is any fun," said Tammy. "But wait until she sees my pictures."

Daddy, Terry, and Tammy went off up the trail.

"Stop, you two," Tammy said. "I want to take a picture of you walking up the trail. Daddy, get behind Terry so the pack will show."

Reprinted from Mary Elizabeth Baker, TAMMY CAMPS IN THE ROCKY MOUNTAINS, by permission of the publisher (Copyright 1970, Houghton-Mifflin Company).

LEVEL 3

There was once an Old Lady who lived in a house on top of a hill. At the foot of the hill was a river, and on the other side of the river was a town.

The Old Lady was never lonely, for she lived with her animal friends:

a Brindle Cat,

a Magic Mouse,

and an alligator

named Alexander.

When the Brindle Cat wasn't sitting in the sun, he was thinking about how to catch the Magic Mouse. But the Magic Mouse had made herself invisible. The Cat couldn't catch her.

LEVEL 4

Louis (Satchmo) Armstrong is credited with making jazz an accepted part of American culture. Born on July 4, 1900, in New Orleans, Louisiana, Armstrong's musical career as trumpeter and vocalist is permanently tied to the history of American jazz. Louis Armstrong took jazz out of New Orleans, where it was born, and introduced it as an art form around the world. He had become a legend in his own lifetime. Wherever New Orleans jazz is played, Stachmo is known and respected as onc of the greatest jazz musicians.

Reprinted from Eldonna L. Everetts, Lyman C. Hunt, Bernard Weiss, TIME TO WONDER, p. 268, by permission of the publisher (Copyright 1973, Holt, Rinehart and Winston, Inc.).

APPENDIX B

PARAGRAPHS FOR SILENT READING

PRIMER LEVEL

"Is that a bird
in the big tree?" said Mike.
"Yes, it is.
A little blue bird."

LEVEL 1

A little brown rabbit lived
with his mother.

They lived in a little home
in the grass.

One day he said, "Mother!
I have no friends close by
to play with me.

Please tell me a story
about a make-believe rabbit.

Let him be a brave little rabbit."

Reprinted from Albert J. Harris, Mae Knight Clark, LANDS OF PLEASURE, p. 154, by permission of the publisher (Copyright 1965-66, The Macmillan Company).

LEVEL 2

Once upon a time there was a man
who was called Rambling Richard.
He was called that because he liked to go
from town to town. He walked and walked
over the earth.

Rambling Richard liked to write.
Every day he tried to write a story.
Sometimes the story was real. Sometimes
it was make-believe. Sometimes it was funny.
Sometimes it was sad. But every day
he tried to write a story.

Reprinted from Albert J. Harris, Mae Knight Clark, Alice M. Scipione, ENCHANTED GATES, p. 153, by permission of the publisher (Copyright 1965-66, The Macmillan Company).

LEVEL 3

Thousands of years ago men had very different ways of fishing than we have today. They caught fish with their hands. They tossed long pointed spears at them. They shot them with bows and arrows.

We have gone a long way from the bow-and-arrow days. Even so, our fishermen still don't haul up enough fish to feed our people. We have to buy fish from other countries. As the years go by, we will need more fish because there will be more people to feed. The number of people in the world keeps on growing.

LEVEL 4

Dinosaurs were the strangest animals that have ever lived. They were the sort of creatures you might dream about in a bad nightmare. The word "dinosaur" means "terrible lizard." The lizards, snakes, and crocodiles of today belong to the same reptile family as these enormous beasts of the past.

Some dinosaurs were so huge, they were heavier than a dozen elephants. Some dinosaurs walked on powerful hind legs and stood as tall as palm trees. Still others had short legs and square bodies and were as big as army tanks. These dinosaurs had long horns and ugly, hooked beaks. Dinosaurs were so strange and terrible that other animals ran from them in fright.

Reprinted from Albert J. Harris, Marion Gartler, Caryl Roman, Marcella Benditt, Dorothy Whittington, THE MAGIC WORD, p. 132, by permission of the publisher (Copyright 1967, The Macmillan Company).

APPENDIX C

SOUNDS

CONSONANTS

b	c	d	f	g	h	j
k	l	m	n	p	q	r
s	t	v	w	x	y	z

VOWELS

a   e   i   o   u

DIGRAPHS

sh   th   wh   ch

BLENDS

dr	fl	wr	fr	tr	br	cl
sl	gl	sw	gr	dw	sm	bl
pl	pr	st	tw	sp		

APPENDIX D

WORDS

WORD LISTS

Level P (Primer)	Level 1	Level 2
are	again	across
at	around	air
away	be	anything
boy	know	back
came	many	beauty
did	next	behind
do	night	build
for	off	cook
girl	other	dress
he	over	floor
like	please	hard
me	their	know
my	thing	noise
no	time	over
one	took	side
red	water	string
some	way	through
they	when	wash

WORD LISTS

Level 3	Level 4
above	balance
also	bound
beautiful	cement
careful	difficult
clothes	educate
different	exercise
empty	fright
fasten	handsome
heard	imagine
hundred	invent
indeed	meantime
invite	popular
kept	rude
lovely	signal
path	suggest
upon	thrill
were	tribe
whole	warmth